PRAISE FOR EVERYDAY GENEROSITY

"Drew is a gifted communicator who has a passion to help families discover the joy of giving. Having known him before he was a teenager, he brings a message on this topic as a teenager that is unique. Who does this at his age? Something is going on here and we all need to listen. This is pretty special. Find out why!"

Emerson Eggerichs
New York Times best-selling author of *Love & Respect*

"I know Drew and have heard him speak on generosity—he shares from his heart and cares deeply about impacting his generation with the life-giving message that it's better to give than receive."

Kirk Cousins
NFL quarterback

"Drew Formsma is one of the youngest authors I know, but he has wisdom beyond his years. And the message of this book is a powerful one: you are never too young to be generous. Get ready to be challenged by this book!"

Mark Batterson
New York Times best-selling author of *The Circle Maker*
Lead pastor of National Community Church

"The Lord calls believers to give—not out of compulsion, but cheerfully. Drew Formsma reminds us that we're called to be obedient and open-handed not just with money, but with all that God entrusts to us."

Jim Daly
President, Focus on the Family

EVERYDAY GENEROSITY

EVERYDAY GENEROSITY

becoming a generous family in a *selfie world*

DREW FORMSMA
BRAD FORMSMA
Award winning author of
I Like Giving –the transforming power of a generous life

Highsmith and Company
Interior Design by Mitchell Shea
Cover design by Laura Formsma and Kierstin Toth

Printed in the United States of America

Print ISBN: 978-1-7326426-0-7
eBook ISBN: 978-1-7326426-1-4

First Edition 19 18 17 16 15 / 10 9 8 7 6 5 4 3 2 1

Dedicated to my mom

Thank you for training me up and showing me my gifts from
God
that I am able to use to help others even at the age of sixteen

And to moms everywhere

You might feel invisible and unappreciated at times,
but know that you truly are valuable to your children

CONTENTS

INTRODUCTION

You're probably wondering, *Is this kid really sixteen years old?* I would be thinking the same thing! I know it's unusual to come across a book actually written by a teenager. In fact, when God used a dream to put the vision in my heart to write a book, I wondered whether I could really pull it off. I'm not one of those people who gets spiritual dreams that often, but this night I was woken up by one. I felt like God wanted to use me to speak to parents and teens about how to create a culture of generosity in families all over the world. I didn't know what to do with that, so I decided to pray and ask God for a clear sign.

A couple days later, I was riding in an Uber, and just a few minutes into the ride the lady asked me, "Hey, is your dad Brad Formsma?"

Slightly uncomfortable and confused, I responded, "Yeah, I hope so."

"That's great!" she said. "His message transformed my life. I heard him speak, and I'm having so much fun with all of these giving experiences."

She told me some of her giving stories, and then she asked me to tell her some of mine. As I finished sharing with her, she said, "You need to write a book. Your dad has inspired me, but I need to get my kids to give and I just don't know where to start. I will be the proudest parent if my son becomes a generous and caring young man. I would love to read a book that could motivate both my kids and me. And having your dad's instruction and ideas would be great too." As we arrived at my destination she asked, "How does that sounds to you?"

"Wow!" I said. "Are you sure you're an Uber driver, or are you an angel from God?" As I got out of the car, I thought, *Uber rides are supposed to be sketchy, not spiritual.* My parents always said don't talk to strangers, but this was a totally different situation. God was using the Uber driver to speak into my life.

If that wasn't enough, the next week I was in another Uber, and an entirely different driver said, "Dude, you need to write a book full of how to start giving and ways to give." At that point, I knew God was confirming my dream, and it was time to get started writing.

Over the next nine months I worked late at night, after doing my schoolwork, to write this book with my dad. He played a key role in the entire process of writing this book with me, bringing along over Fifteen years of experience in studying and speaking on generosity, as well as finances, friends, and the belief that God was with us. He's simply an expert.

As I have worked with my dad, I have met many more parents longing for something that will help train kind, caring, and generous kids—kids who look outside of themselves and their selfie-driven, me-centric world.

For a long time I was like every other kid—selfish.

I wrote this book determined to help define and discover what generosity looks like in a kid's life. What I've found is that it doesn't matter if we have five dollars or five million dollars; we all have an opportunity to give every day. We have the opportunity to become aware and step through the door God has opened for us. I believe we can turn hate and hurt into kindness and generosity for everyone we come in contact with every day. The goal is to get as many people as possible to start looking outside of themselves. Our role is to let God work through us and let generosity be the headline in our lives.

You may be thinking, *How can a sixteen-year-old do justice to the vast topic of generosity?* Well, first and most important, I have interacted with the Bible and read God's Word, which speaks about generosity thousands of times. This is the core of my inspiration because I know it's God's message. And while I certainly reference a handful of Bible verses throughout the book, I want you to know that the Bible is loaded with a lot more to say about generosity and money.

I have also had the rare opportunity to observe many givers and discuss this great subject with hundreds of people across America. Part of this book is the result of my dad sharing his platform speaking time with me along with many of his friends who are leading business owners or pastors and recognized as being generous. I am so grateful to have had a front-row seat to learn from so many great people!

In the following pages, you will pick up insights from my family and many other generous people. My hope is that this book will challenge, encourage, inspire, and motivate you to live a lifestyle of generosity!

CHAPTER 1

What Is Generosity?

The first time I spoke in front of a lot of people was on March 14, 2015, when I was in seventh grade. This was a big deal because I was speaking to the junior high group at my church and many of my classmates were in the room. I was really excited because I was happy to have the opportunity to share my heart in front of my peers.

Many of the adults asked me, "Did you get nervous standing up there in front of your friends and their parents?" I told them I didn't get nervous a bit! I loved having the opportunity to speak and encourage people to do more for others and create a generous world. And after that moment, I knew that part of God's plan for me was to speak to students and parents about living generously.

From the time I was in middle school, my dad would take me along with him as he traveled to this meeting or that conference. My dad, Brad Formsma, founded an organization called I Like Giving, and he speaks on generosity to large groups of people around the country. By having me with him, he was letting me meet his friends and we were building a special relationship. I love going to different places and meeting new people. My first time speaking with him was at a church in Petoskey, Michigan. We had gone there for him to speak and he surprised me by asking, "Hey, Drew, would you ever want to share a giving story?"

I grinned. "Dad, I have been waiting for you to ask me!"

So, when we got into the meeting and my dad started his talk, I thought, *I hope he really does call me up to share my giving story.* A little later in the program, I saw him look at me and knew it was my time to shine. The truth is, I was more worried about tripping up the stairs than speaking. Once I made it up the stairs (safely), I shared a story I call "I Like Bed Bath & Beyond," about a giving opportunity that had actually come up while I was on this trip with him.

I had been with my dad at Bed Bath & Beyond getting two pillows because the ones we had at the hotel were bricks and I had been having some neck problems. It was like a candy store in there, with so many different kinds of pillows to choose from, so we asked one of the salespeople how to know which to choose. We described what we were looking for, and she knew the exact pillow we needed because she had similar problems. She pointed us toward one particular top-of-the-line pillow. I grabbed two of them, and the saleswoman led us up front to the register so that she could check us out. Then my dad whispered to me to grab a third pillow, and at that moment I realized we were going to buy the saleswoman the pillow she had been hoping to get for herself.

We got up to the counter and the saleswoman scanned the first two pillows. When she scanned the last one and started to put it in our bag, we told her, "This pillow is for you!" She almost fainted right there, and everyone around us was picking up on that rush you experience from giving and receiving. The clerk behind her said, "Whoa, you must have done a good job!"

After a moment of shock, the saleswoman said, "You made my day," and then repeated it a couple more times.

I walked out of there with the biggest smile. And, that night, as I lay my head on my new pillow, I couldn't stop thinking of the lady we blessed earlier in the day. I can promise you one thing: I had one great night of sleep!

After I shared this story at the church, a man from the back of the auditorium stood up and yelled, "I was there! I am the manager at that Bed Bath & Beyond, and we have been talking about this since it happened! Our whole team is so excited; there is so much energy. My employee said she hasn't had someone do something nice for her in thirty years!"

I was floored. That had definitely never happened before in all the times my dad has spoken, and I felt God was telling me to keep sharing my story. So, the next month I asked my dad if I could share another giving story at the next church, and he said yes. I am so thankful that my parents have always been there to support me and give me the opportunities I need to succeed, because I never would have been on that stage if my dad hadn't given me the chance.

From that point on, I have gone with my dad as often as possible when he speaks around the country, and I always look forward to the chance to speak. I believe my calling is to make sure my generation is known as the Generous Generation, not the iPhone Generation.

When I speak, I try to address the high school and middle school students through a twenty-minute keynote, and then I share a quick giving story with the parents. I'm just getting started, but I believe this is an important message and we will continue to be led to the right places to share it.

The most important reason I want to do this with my dad is that there are a lot of misconceptions about giving that keep people from choosing to live generously. I think this is especially true for my generation, so I want to go out and set an example for them so they can see how easy and rewarding it really is.

In addition to the speaking, I wanted to write this book because I see it as the best way to reach all the people who need to hear the message that I won't be able to share with them personally. Another reason is that I have the perspective that we only have today. A few years ago, my dad was diagnosed with a rare form of leukemia and given twenty-four months to live. This reminded me that each day matters, and between the speaking and writing, I saw it all as an opportunity to spend quality time with my dad.

Maybe you are reading this book because you have read my dad's book, *I Like Giving.* Maybe someone gave it to you as a gift. Hopefully, you are giving this message (and me) a chance because you sense that living generously is something that will make a big, positive difference in your life and you want to know more. In any case, I hope you will find a few answers and the inspiration you need here to help you start making generosity a part of your everyday life.

GENEROSITY FOR GENERATIONS: SEVEN WAYS TO A GENEROUS LIFE

My dad's grandpa taught him that generosity is beyond just giving money. One Friday afternoon when Dad was twelve years old, his grandpa called him.

"Bradley," he said, "I will pick you up on Saturday morning and take you to my bakery to bake sixteen loaves of bread."

Dad's grandpa owned a large commercial bakery and his test kitchen was next to his office where he would make small batches of bread. My dad was so excited as he thought of all the fresh sliced bread and jam that he would eat that Saturday morning. Well, his grandpa had a different plan in mind. After the loaves of bread cooled off, they loaded them into the trunk of his car.

At their first stop Great-Grandpa gave two fresh loaves of bread and several kind and affirming words to a widow that he knew from church. He was modeling how to be generous with words.

My dad was hoping the second stop would be to sample that fresh bread, yet this time Great-Grandpa gave away several more loaves of bread along with a white envelope that contained a check. This time Great-Grandpa was modeling being generous with money.

As they drove down the road my dad kept hoping that soon they would pull the car over and enjoy that fresh bread! Well, not so fast. At the next stop, several more loaves of bread came from the trunk of the car and Great-Grandpa was giving someone a letter of referral to help him get a job because of the connections my great-grandpa had. This time he was being generous with influence.

My dad shared how he slowly got the point that this particular Saturday morning was about his grandpa modeling the generous life. The next stop was Great-Grandpa spending time with a person who couldn't leave their home. You guessed it—generous with time.

The following stop he gave his full attention to a retired employee whose wife was very sick. He was showing my dad the power of being generous with his attention.

The last stop and the remaining loaves of bread were given with Great-Grandpa sharing a tool that someone needed to use. "Sharing with others the things we have is a powerful way to give," Great-Grandpa would always say!

As my dad looked back on his experiences with his grandpa later in life, he realized that his grandpa was modeling for him the seven ways to live a generous life: being generous with our thoughts, words, money, time, influence, attention, and possessions.

THOUGHTS

Generous with our thoughts might be hard to understand. Oftentimes we can make assumptions and judgments about a person without reason. The way we think about someone or something can be either kind or hateful. We truly never know what someone is going through. They could be acting unfavorable because they found out they had cancer, lost a family member, or just failed a test. Someone being thoughtful and empathetic to their circumstance could be the difference in their response to their situation. Instead of thinking whether someone needs your generosity, think about the impact of your one decision. Most people just want to be thought of and heard from.

Our family was recently at a conference. One of my dad's longtime friends was also there and yet they missed talking to each other because of the busy schedule and commitments that my dad's friend had going on. They would pass each other briefly in the hallway and smile or nod their head, and yet they never had a chance to catch up on what was happening in each other's lives. As we flew home my dad shared how he was having negative thoughts that were not his own. They were thoughts that his friend was mad at him or that he had done something to offend this friend. He shared how he prayed that he would extend grace and that he would give the benefit of the doubt and see the best in his friend. He mentioned that he needed to pray this through over and over again until he got peace in his heart.

Four days after the conference ended, his friend texted him and apologized that they had not been able to connect and that he greatly appreciated their long friendship. Due to three major issues going on in his life, he had been greatly distracted. Prior to learning this, my dad had thought about confronting his friend, yet his early thoughts were so negative he realized that he could have damaged the friendship by allowing his less-than-generous thoughts to control the situation.

We all can benefit from being generous with our thoughts, and the more we become aware of what we are thinking about, the more we can live to give the benefit of the doubt and to see the best in people—even if that means praying and waiting for the situation to work itself out.

WORDS

One generous word can change someone's whole day. People just want to feel known and recognized. The weight of our words is more than we think. The words we use to another could make or break their day. Can you remember the times when someone affirmed you? A time that you were complimented or encouraged? I bet you remember many of those times. Sometimes being generous with our words is for people we are very close to in life. Other times it's for people who every day serve our country and our communities. It may mean thanking those who have a thankless job.

Like Conrad.

My dad travels to speak at leading businesses and churches across the country, which requires him to go through a lot of airports. Now anyone who travels knows that a clean airport bathroom is a huge bonus. One day as my dad was leaving the cleanest airport bathroom he had ever used, he got that nudge to give a kind word to the man who had just cleaned it. As my dad introduced himself to the worker and they exchanged names, he noticed that the worker's name patch was blank. After learning the man's name was Conrad, my dad said, "Conrad, if you worked for me your name would be on your shirt. You matter. I think you're a good man."

My dad saw a little tear well up in the corner of the man's eye. My dad floated away and caught up with my mom. She said, "You're glowing! What happened?"

My dad said, "I just met Conrad, the guy who cleans the bathrooms. I had the greatest conversation with him. I thought I was doing the giving and yet I received so much joy from giving him a kind word."

MONEY

It doesn't matter if you're giving ten dollars or ten million dollars, a financial gift is often connected to our heart. I give to my church, yet I also try and find other nonprofits to give to that I feel relate to me and my passion. Mr. David Green of Hobby Lobby shared with me that the habits I'm making now will be similar to the ones I have in fifty years. He encouraged me to give financially now even with a small amount because the habit will live on. When I do have a steady paycheck and make good money, I won't have to struggle in making the decision to give because I made it already during my teenager years. And in times of hardship and being tight on money I will give because that decision was made already.

One day I told my dad that I was looking for a good place to invest money on a regular basis. I told him I wanted to give to something that was effective and had been proven to be a good organization. The look on his face told me that he was a little surprised to hear me use the word *invest*. That's exactly what we are doing when we give—investing in God's work and the lives of others. He told me to get my antenna working, which is his favorite line to get me looking, listening, and asking questions to find the next giving opportunity.

The following day I had the chance to attend a meeting with my dad and fourteen businesspeople, including the aforementioned founder of Hobby Lobby, Mr. David Green. It was a huge privilege to hear Mr. Green's views on giving, and I have to say it was one of those days I will never forget. At one point Mart Green (David's son) shared a story that changed his life.

He was on a trip across the world to deliver a Bible that had been translated into Eastern Jakalteko. After a crazy long journey, he arrived for the presentation of the newly translated Bible. A man named Gaspar came forward to get his new Bible and he wept. This was a life-changing moment for Mart. But Mart's experience impacted me as well.

How many Bibles do I have access to? I can access God's Word on my YouVersion Bible app in so many translations. I know I have never wept getting a Bible. As Mart shared the number of languages that have yet to receive a Bible in their language, he mentioned how many translating agencies were combining forces to share their best practices and to not duplicate work. And then he said, "For thirty-five dollars, a single verse can be translated each month."

It hit me—here was the investment I had just been asking my dad about! That day I went to the Illuminations website and decided that I could translate two verses each month. I am excited that I can play a small part in helping bring God's Word to people like Gaspar—twenty-four verses each year!

TIME

In a world that has become faster and faster, it seems like it's become harder and harder to be generous with our time. It takes intentionality to give your time. One day my dad said to my brother and me that we were going to go on a surprise ride. Well, we piled into his car and drove down the road for what seemed like forever. We didn't know where we were going and were kind of anxious to find out what we were going to get out of this surprise ride experience. We pulled into a great big building that had flags lining the driveway, and we started asking Dad, "Where are we? What are we doing at this big building?"

As we parked the car my dad explained to us that we were at a veterans' facility. He told us that we were going to go inside and look for someone we could strike up a conversation with and spend some time with that afternoon. Well, there was a man in a wheelchair who was headed out the door to smoke and we asked him if we could go with him. As we stood next to his wheelchair he pointed at a huge American flag hanging between two large oak trees in the middle of the lawn. He asked us, "Do you know what that flag stands for?" Then he answered his own question. "That flag stands for freedom!" he exclaimed.

He said every morning he goes out to salute the flag and smoke a cigarette all alone. But this day was different. He said, "Why are you guys here?"

"I wanted to come here with my boys today and spend some time with one of the great heroes of our country," my dad said.

A big smile broke across this old soldier's face, and as we said our goodbyes and walked away he yelled at the top of his lungs, "You made my day!"

The three of us stopped in our tracks, turned around, and yelled back, "You made ours!"

My grandma also modeled generosity to me. One day, I was spending some time with her, and she suggested that we visit her long-time elder at the rest home. I could tell that this elder meant a lot to her, so we went and spent hours with this ninety-eight-year-old lady named Lavon.

My grandma had been visiting Lavon for over ten years. She would bring Lavon food, take her out, and love on her. As Lavon was blind, my grandma would also bring her audio books and often read to her. Sitting there, I realized that Lavon would be so lonely without the generosity of my grandma and her weekly visits. The joy on Lavon's face when we sat with her was overwhelming to see. No money could buy what my grandma was giving to her. All people want is to feel known and cared for. She loved it so much that she wanted us to stay the night.

As my grandma would oftentimes bring visitors with her, including friends and grandchildren, she was modeling generosity to everyone she brought with her to the rest home. I believe that when we are generous with our time we truly understand who a generous person really is. Someone who serves and takes the spotlight off of themselves and places it onto others instead.

INFLUENCE

Generosity with our influence could make all the difference in someone's life. Everyone has influence. When I was twelve years old my dad told me that he and his friends had decided to help a man named William who had just moved from Nigeria. He was a janitor at a museum trying to save enough money to buy a used van. My dad and his friends delivered the van to William, and he was overjoyed. Now not only would he be able to get to work in a timely way, but he also could now lead a Bible study at a local jail. And his six kids would now have a place to sit!

A few months later my dad asked William how things were going at the jail.

"Well, there's a little bit of a problem," William said.

"What is it?" Dad asked.

"I don't have a driver's license," William admitted.

My dad was shocked. He didn't see that one coming!

"Yes," William said, "I continue to go to this place where they keep charging me to take the test and I keep failing."

My dad decided to go with him to the test center and soon realized that because of his language barrier the Department of Motor Vehicles was sending him to an outside contractor who was taking advantage of his poor English. He realized that William needed somebody with influence to help him get his driver's license. My dad was able to bring his influence and ability to communicate with the people who ran the driver's test agency, holding them accountable and keeping them honest so that William was able to get his license. With his license William was then able to visit the jail, bring his family to church, and get a better, more flexible schedule.

As I look at my life, the best example of someone who has been generous with his or her influence is my dad. In fact, he shared his influence with me, giving me the opportunity to share that first giving story on stage. His trust that I wouldn't mess up or do anything dumb was amazing to watch. I could have said something that could mess up his whole career, but he trusted in me.

Now, trust is built over time; it's a process. I have felt like God has given me a message and my dad trusts what God is doing. Through his relationship and connections, he has opened me up to the most amazing people. And he has done the same for my siblings and so many of his friends.

Sharing your influence is helping someone get somewhere they couldn't get on their own. I see my dad introduce people to others without expecting to get anything from it. Your connection could be abused, but if you get the nudge go for it, even if it doesn't make sense at first.

ATTENTION

Being generous with our attention is tricky. If you are having a conversation with someone and become distracted by what is going on over your shoulder, it might seem you don't care about who you are talking to. It can be so difficult to not be interrupted by something else but to give your full, undivided attention to the person in front of you.

I was at a conference and ran into the CEO of Southwest Airlines. I walked up and introduced myself and we talked for ten minutes. The amazing part is that though there were several people around us, the whole time he was locked in on me. This leading influencer in today's society was generous with his attention, and it made me feel like I was worthy to be talking to him even at my age. I look at the culture in his company today and it carries the same legacy of being generous in all circumstances. I oftentimes catch myself being distracted by my phone or another person, but really, I just need to be in the moment with who I'm with. When we are distracted while talking to someone, our nonverbal communication tells them that they're not good enough to be talking to.

Next time you are with someone, try giving them your full attention and see what happens. It might be hard at first, but as you start the habit of being fully engaged it should become easier.

POSSESSIONS

Sharing our possessions is a huge deal. It seems so easy but can be challenging. It's easy to share a few eggs with the neighbor when they run short while they are making chocolate cookies. But when the neighbor's car stops working and they ask if they can use your brand-new SUV, that's when it can be a little harder to be generous. I like to remind myself every day that everything I have is God's and if he gives me an opportunity to share I should lean into that and do it!

When I lived in Michigan we had a house with a lower level that was completely finished with several bedrooms, a kitchen, and a bath. My parents made a point of looking for opportunities to let people live with us who were in between jobs or houses. The way our house was designed allowed the people living downstairs to use a back staircase to come in and out of the house so that they could feel like they had their own privacy. I was so excited to have other people in our house that I would sneak down the staircase to see them, which was very fun for me and a little stressful for my mom because she couldn't always find me. I remember thinking this must be what everybody does—sharing rooms in their house with people that they have met either through other friends or at church. One time my dad became frustrated because he let one of the families park in the garage and their car leaked oil all over the garage floor. This was good for me to see, because sometimes when we share things we may not get them back, or sometimes you'll end up with that stain on the garage floor!

Another time, some people were staying at our home and they decided to play the guitar late into the night. That was also one of those things that we all needed to forgive and then move on.

GIVING IN THE TOUGH TIMES

I will never forget the Christmas of 2012. My dad and mom were cleaning out my sister's play room when one of the large toys fell on his foot, which caused it to bleed and the next day it got infected. This landed my dad in the hospital over Christmas. It was a total downer as we couldn't visit him because the hospital had a pneumonia outbreak! Several days later his white blood cell counts slowly dropped so they discharged him from the hospital. As the months went on my dad had to continue to get his blood monitored. One day his doctor called to tell him that he needed to see a hematologist. After further testing my dad was diagnosed with leukemia. I remember the day that I walked past our home office where my mom and dad were crying. My mom was really upset and my dad had a very serious look on his face.

They waited a week before telling us kids what was going on. The mood in our house was heavy. My mom looked sad most of the time.

One beautiful sunny day that spring my dad and I were kayaking at his friend's lake house. I was in the back of the kayak and said, "Dad, could you die from that thing with your blood?"

He waited for what felt like an hour and said, "Yes—I could."

I said, "Dad, I don't think you are going to die because I think God has work for you to do by encouraging people to live generously through *I Like Giving*."

I don't often talk like that—especially when I was ten years old—but I really meant it!

My dad underwent chemotherapy for several years, and after we moved to California he started to see a doctor at UCLA. One day the doctor told him that he was not able to detect the disease. We were so excited and thanked God for a miraculous healing. Still, we were told that he would have to continue chemotherapy for the rest of his life.

Since then I have gone with my dad several times to UCLA to get his blood checked and it seems like there is always a giving story that comes out of those trips. The guy has made the generous life such a part of everyday life, it's fun to watch and see what will happen next.

GENEROUS IN EVERY SITUATION

One day the nurse taking his blood was in a grumpy mood. Her name was Joy. (Seriously, some people just have the wrong name for the job!) My dad asked Joy if she ever went with a friend to Starbucks and got the 910-calorie drink with all the whipped cream and drizzle on top. She looked at him kind of peculiar and said, "I guess I would." Well, as she was labeling up his blood he slid a Starbucks gift card on her chair. As he and I left the lab he said, "Hey, Joy, have fun with your friend." She glanced over to her chair, saw the gift card, and a huge smile broke across her face.

Walking down the hallway my dad said, "It's just better to give than receive." The interesting part was that even though I was only observing the generosity, I too was experiencing the joy of it.

GENEROUS TO EVERYONE

The day the doctor told my dad he was going to take him off of chemotropic my dad said, "Doc, it's a miracle!" to which the doctor said, "Those don't happen," and then he complimented my dad's shoes. Seriously, he transitioned straight from miracles to shoes. So, my dad said, "What size are your shoes? Size 10?" His doctor said, "You think you are so smart! They are size 9.5."

My dad then thought to himself, *Yes, actually I am smart. I just learned your shoe size.* He went straight to the store where he had bought his shoes and bought the 9.5 for his doctor. Who does this? My dad. He wrote a note to the doctor along with the shoes, which said, "Dear Doc, thank you for using your God-given gifts to help a guy like me stay around a little longer." And then he closed the note with, "These shoes will help you be one step more like me!"

The funny thing is that when the doctor got the shoes in the mail he called my dad and said, "You are crazy but thanks for the shoes."

"Yes, I do," Dad agreed.

What is generosity? My great-grandpa showed the seven ways of being generous to my grandma and my dad, and now my grandma and dad are modeling generosity to me. Generosity is not just about being generous with your money. It's about being generous with your thoughts, words, time, attention, influence, and possessions—no matter what's going on in your own life, no matter what situation you are in, and no matter who you are with.

That's generosity.

CHAPTER 2
What's Holding You Back?

We can come up with many excuses for why we aren't living generously, but that's all they are . . . excuses. I'm going to list some of the most common ones I hear.

Do any of these excuses sound familiar to you?

I'm too young.

Age really doesn't matter when it comes to living generously. In fact, the younger you start, the better, because it becomes a way of life early on, and you have many more years of getting to change people's lives. Whether you are eight or ninety-eight, there is always something you can give and some way you can be generous.

My parents really encouraged us to live generously and they modeled that for my siblings and me. One day, my brother and I were thinking about how we could be generous. How could we make an impact? At the time, I was ten and he was fourteen; we decided to have a lemonade stand and donate all the money we got that day to Compassion International. We made over one hundred dollars, and even though we were sitting out in the hot, humid summer weather, it was so fun to think that we were helping others in another country.

My brother and I have had many lemonade stands, but this one I'll never forget because we were earning to help others instead of ourselves. When we live generously, it makes a huge difference for the giver *and* the receiver.

It doesn't matter what age you are; you can always live generously and be others-focused. Pick out something you know how to do and then think about how you can use that to help someone else.

I don't have any money to give.

You don't need to be rich to give. Did you know that people who have close to nothing are often the ones who give the most (as a percentage of what they have) and give the most often? As shared in the previous chapter, generosity isn't only about money; it also comes through our words, actions, wisdom, and personal gifts.

Many people say, "I'm not rich enough to give," and I say, "That's okay. You can share a kind word with a friend or help an elderly person carry their groceries to their car. It's really that simple." Once, I was sitting in my seat on an airplane and saw an elderly woman coming down the aisle to her seat. All the passengers seemed focused on themselves and didn't notice her. So I stood up and asked, "Can I help you with your luggage?" She was so grateful, and as I lifted her suitcase into the overhead bin, she said, "Your parents must be proud." I went back to my seat thankful that I saw a need and could help.

Generosity isn't just about money; it's about seeing beyond yourself and doing for others.

The next time you notice someone who could use a helping hand, go ahead and step up. It will make you feel great to know you lightened someone else's load.

I don't have time to give.

Generosity isn't just one single act; it's a lifestyle. That may sound time-consuming, but when we make giving part of our lives, it soon becomes second nature and isn't as hard to do. This means we become aware of our surroundings as we begin to notice when people have needs.

If we find time to watch our favorite TV shows, play video games, go shopping, and have dinner out with friends, why can't we also find time for giving? Don't get me wrong; those things are important too. But while we are making time for them, we can surely find five minutes for someone else.

Make it a habit to begin looking for generosity opportunities within the fun things you do for yourself. It's an easy way to combine two things that will make you feel good.

It doesn't really matter if I'm generous.

It might be tempting to pass off the responsibility of giving to others and hope someone else will help a person in need. It's true, there probably will be someone else to come along and pick up the slack, but when you pass up an opportunity to give, you aren't just delaying that person having their need met; you are cheating yourself out of a chance to fill your own life with joy and happiness. We will go into more detail about the benefits you receive from a generous life later, but it's important to know that giving always makes a difference in the lives of the giver *and* the receiver.

One of my early memories of giving as a family was when we bought bikes for a son and father whose bikes were stolen. The bike was the son's toy and the dad's was his transportation to work. Because their story got a lot of attention in the local media, my mom thought hundreds of people would have donated by the time we heard about it. When we got to their house, though, there was not one bike in the front yard. If we had stayed home and said, "What difference does it make to be generous?" they might not have had their needs met, and we would have lost an opportunity to bring joy and excitement into our own lives.

The next time you think it doesn't matter if you give, try putting yourself in the other person's shoes and imagine how it would feel if you had a need and everyone assumed it didn't matter if they did anything to help. Then think about what kind of a difference it would make in your life to have someone show generosity to you.

It's not the right time.

An easy excuse for delaying action is that you don't think the time is right. But you have to ask yourself, "Is there ever going to be a right time? Will I ever run out of reasons to put off doing something for someone else?" As my dad battled cancer and thought about death and what might happen to our family, he was still able to be kind and generous to the men and women at the clinic where he was getting treatment, such as when he gave the Starbucks card to Joy.

It's always the right time to be generous in some way. If you are constantly worrying about what you have to do, or where you have to go, you never will get around to being generous. But it's not about you; it's about others! The next time you find yourself thinking, *I can't do anything for others right now*, stop and take a look around you to see if someone else is also in need and try to find a way to help. Even if it's just a kind word, you'll be amazed at how it will change their day and your perspective as well.

It feels weird to do something for others.

There is always some risk involved in stepping outside your comfort zone. And, in many cases, the person you feel led to help is going to be a stranger. Of course, that's going to feel weird. In fact, you might be led to help someone who doesn't like you. It reminds me of the story Jesus tells in the Bible about the Samaritan who helped the man who was beaten and robbed. Samaritans were looked down on by other Jews back then, and this man could have gone on his way and ignored the man in need, like others had done. The Samaritan could have thought it would be weird to stop and help this guy. Instead he went above and beyond to make sure this guy was taken care of, and it made a huge difference in both of their lives. Jesus gave us the example of how to live generously and when to live generously, which is all the time in every way we can.

The next time you feel like you should do something for someone and you hesitate, ask yourself, "How would I feel if I needed something and no one helped because they thought it was weird?"

My gift won't make a difference.

It just isn't true that your giving won't make a difference. First, your generosity will always have an impact, whether on the person who receives or on you as the giver. We will go into more detail in later chapters about all the benefits of giving and receiving, but it is important to understand that generosity changes the lives of everyone involved, even if you don't always get to see the results immediately (and sometimes not ever).

I attended a camp one summer, and all week I was becoming more and more aware of how hard this elderly nurse worked to hand out the medication to several campers. On the last day of camp, I was walking to the dining hall and saw her in the distance. I looked closer and realized her arms were full of boxes, and she was holding on to a service dog too! In a split second, I made the decision to do something to help this woman. As I ran down to help her, I noticed many people walking right past. I asked her if I could carry the boxes for her. She said, "Oh my gosh, yes, thank you! I thought I was going to drop the medicine boxes everywhere." It was such a simple act of generosity to take a few steps out of my way, but it made a big difference for her.

You may think what you have to give won't make a difference because it's not a big deal, or because you think it won't be noticed. Instead, try putting yourself in the shoes of the recipient and ask yourself, "Would this make a difference to me? Would someone doing this for me change my attitude, lighten my load, or turn my day around?" I think you'll find your answer.

They just want my money.

I believe the best form of giving happens when you do so out of the goodness of your heart, not out of duty or obligation. There have been times when I have seen TV commercials for charities that show small kids from other countries who are unhealthy and have flies swarming around them. It really pulls at my heartstrings and it frustrates me to see others around the world having such great struggles. I've learned there are some organizations that manipulate people and play on their emotions to get people to give. To me, that is not cheerful giving; that is forced giving. I know at times people have been taken advantage of, and that can affect their willingness to be generous in the future. To me, this kind of experience is like crust building up around a person's heart—messy giving leaves behind bad feelings, and after a few times, this residue can begin to harden around a person's heart. The scary thing about the crust is that people don't even realize they have it because it builds up slowly over time.

A few years ago, I learned a technique called "flipping the scenario," which teaches you to take a negative experience and try to find something positive about it. If I let a few messy giving experiences affect me, it will steal the joy of giving. If I can find another way to look at the situation and find some gift in it, I can avoid having past messy giving experiences negatively affect me. Of course, that doesn't mean I will continue to allow others to abuse my generosity, but I can use these experiences to learn more about asking questions and understanding more about the organization or person I give to, instead of deciding I won't give at all.

If you are concerned about the integrity of an organization requesting a donation, check one of the websites that rate charities and do some research to find out if they are trustworthy. If you are dealing with an individual, ask around or just trust your gut. Sometimes you might end up the victim of a scam, but you have to trust that God will turn that situation into something good somewhere down the road.

They are just going to take advantage of me.

Maybe you've found yourself thinking something like: *They will use the gift in a way I didn't intend for it to be used; They are going to just keep coming back for more;* or, *They are just using me.* The reality of dealing with human beings is that not everyone is going to have good intentions.

I have found myself in situations where someone took advantage of me. One of those times was when I gave money to a homeless man and I saw the unfortunate way he used it. I watched him head straight to a liquor store to buy alcohol. I felt very disappointed by how he chose to use the money I gave him. But I made a decision that day to keep giving because I wasn't going to let the homeless man take the joy of giving out of my life. Then I told my dad about that experience and he said we have to be careful with judging these situations because oftentimes we can "waste money" ourselves.

This kind of situation can cast a shadow over all of our other giving, but we don't want that to happen! Oftentimes people will ask me about whether you should give to a panhandler. The answer is if you feel the nudge then do it, and remember that those experiences are only a tiny percentage of all the giving opportunities you will encounter.

Most of the people I talk to who feel their generosity has been abused have simply stopped giving. But that is a very lonely (and, honestly, selfish) life. The idea of never giving again because someone took advantage of you is crazy because the odds are really good that there has been, or will be, a time when you have done the same to someone else. Maybe you spent your birthday money on a game you knew your parents wouldn't approve of. Or maybe your sister helped you with chores and you didn't help with hers. The bottom line is that we can't control how others are going to use the things we give them. All we can do is hope that our act of generosity will inspire them to choose better in the future, and then use these experiences to help you learn discernment.

Instead of refusing to give, work on strengthening your discernment muscle by asking questions and learning other people's stories. If you are still skeptical, ask someone you trust for their input.

AFTER ALL THE EXCUSES

In *I Like Giving,* my dad shares the story of Evelyn, which he called "I Like Being 98." That story told Evelyn's incredible independence at ninety-eight years old and how she found ways to be of service to others even with her limitations. I would like to tell you the rest of the story because it illustrates what happens—how your life changes and expands—when you get past all the excuses and let generosity become a way of life.

Faithful Giving

I had come into the kitchen and overheard my dad explaining to my mom that his accountant was telling him he would not be getting a tax deduction for helping Evelyn. He told my mom, "I care about bearing another person's burden much more than a tax deduction!" I, of course, had to ask, "What's a tax deduction?"

My dad explained how taxes work and how charitable giving can help reduce the amount of taxes you have to pay. It made me realize how giving opens up conversations that you might not have otherwise. On this occasion, my dad was able to share how he was stretched financially by additional gifts he wanted to give, such as when Evelyn's car tires blew up and the brakes went bad. He explained, "Drew, this is someone's mom . . . someone's grandma." He said that even though these are gifts of inconvenience, he felt he had to do it. He called a dealership and got a fair deal, and then he coordinated the drop-off and pickup as well, so Evelyn could get new tires.

Learning this from my dad made me want to get involved as well, and we continued our generosity with Evelyn. We brought her chocolates and just sat and talked with her. These times made such a difference for her, maybe even more than the financial help my dad gave her, because we took an interest in her and gave her our time and attention. My dad said he looked at it as an opportunity to get in on an adventure.

When you redefine how you see generosity, you can be open to the endless possibilities. After Evelyn went to heaven, my parents told me something they had never shared with anyone. Toward the end of her life, Evelyn needed to go into a nursing home. Because she didn't have any money, it looked like the only option was a government-run facility where she would have to share a room with a stranger. My dad couldn't stand the idea of this happening, so he told her to pick the place where she wanted to spend her last days and he would figure out a way for her to go there. It was a place called Green Acres (to me, it seriously sounded like a farm). The cost each month was eight hundred dollars. My dad told her, "Evelyn, I will see this through. I will never leave you."

My dad told me that as he began to calculate his promise, he thought, *I appreciate some risk in my life, but this is a new level of faith at $9,600 a year!* But, he said, as he sent the first check to Green Acres, he had incredible peace. Three weeks later, Evelyn went to heaven and Green Acres never cashed that first check. My dad was tested; and, in my view, he passed! Evelyn's funeral was packed because she too had lived a life of generosity and touched so many lives. You see, for us and for Evelyn, giving wasn't about the money; it was about the relationships.

Living generously can take you from something as simple as offering a kind word to someone or as complex as covering a large expense for them. It isn't necessarily going to be an easy way to approach life, but it will be the most rewarding way you can live. There will always be excuses if you are looking for them, but if you are willing to see things from the other person's perspective, your attitude about giving will change dramatically.

CHAPTER 3
Where Do I Start?

We've talked about what generosity is, what's in it for us as the givers, and why we should be generous. If you're still with me, it means you are interested in living a generous life, and you probably have a lot more questions. I'm going to try to answer the most common questions as we move through the book, but I'm guessing this may be the next question you have: "If I'm going to live generously, how do I get started?"

Most people like to think they would be generous, given the opportunity—and I believe most would—but living generously isn't just about waiting around for an opportunity and then responding to it. It's about looking for opportunities to be generous as you go about your daily life. Starting to live generously requires a process I've broken down into four steps: (1) Reset, (2) Rethink, (3) Remove, and (4) Remember. These steps will help you change the way you think about giving and set your mind in the right direction for making it a lifestyle.

GETTING STARTED WITH THE FOUR *R*'S

Reset is the first part of the process for being successful in changing your approach to generosity. The misconceptions we covered in chapter 1 demonstrate a lot of the wrong thinking that keeps people from giving, and these are ideas that are often shaped over many years of bad situations, incorrect information, or lack of experience. When we do a reset on our attitude about giving, we see it in a different light; we get excited about looking for chances to be generous. Changing old habits and attitudes around giving can be difficult and will take determination to change; once you start, the momentum that comes from the positive feelings you experience will make it easier to keep going.

Rethink is the next step, and it happens when you've reset your attitude and you experience a change in your view of giving. You start to believe that this is how you were made to live. You begin to think that living generously is something you want to practice. What I have experienced is that when my mind changed, my heart began to soften and change as well. You may face challenges in changing your thinking around giving, but don't be discouraged. Remember, it is a process, and lifestyle changes don't happen overnight. I want to encourage you to keep at it!

Remove is the third step, and it involves two of the obstacles that stand in the way. First, you need to remove the excuses from your vocabulary. As we laid out in chapter 1, all the misconceptions that lead to excuses *not to give* just don't hold up. The next things to remove are the naysayers. Of course, I don't mean anything harmful to these folks. Don't minimize the impact they can have on your transition into the generous life. These are the people who either discourage you from giving or, at least, don't support you in your desire to do so. They haven't gotten the memo on what it means to the whole world when we choose to live generously. Removing these obstacles may feel tough in some situations, but what you replace them with will be more rewarding than you can imagine.

And lastly, *remember*, giving isn't about what you can get, but about what you can give. This will help you remember that, no matter what happens with your giving, your intentions— your reasons—came from a good place. Remember that many people like to give but not receive. Someone might block your generosity, but don't let that affect your willingness. As my dad says, "Smile your way through the gift giving; it almost always turns out well!" The great thing about how we are made is that we are wired for generosity, so it doesn't take a lot of effort to remember the good that comes from it.

GETTING STARTED FOR KIDS

I know it probably feels overwhelming as a kid to think about where you can start living generously. One of the reasons I've written this book is to help you understand what generosity means and where to start. If you are feeling inspired and want to start doing something right this minute, even before you finish reading, here are some pointers:

WAYS TO START LIVING GENEROUSLY NOW

1. Look for someone sitting alone and ask if you can join them.
2. Give a genuine compliment to someone for doing good work.

3. Give a smile to someone who seems to be having a bad day.
4. Help carry someone's groceries.
5. Volunteer at a place where you can make a difference— and do it because you want to do it, not because you have to do it.
6. Give a part of your allowance or work money to a nonprofit you believe in.
7. Be kind with your words to friends and peers.
8. Give the mail carrier, gardener, and/or public service workers a drink or a snack and thank them for what they do. (My garbage man loves this one.)
9. Shake the hand of a police officer and/or military personnel and thank them for their service.
10. Have a spirit of service and be helpful—open the door, let someone go before you in line, and so on.

These are just a few ways that you can begin to live the generous life.

Now that we are on the right track with our thoughts, let's talk about how to get started with our actions. One of the best ways to figure out where to start is to watch other generous people doing what they do. Hopefully, your parents are modeling the generous lifestyle and you can follow their example. Kids tend to follow their parents' lead in most aspects of life. One of my dad's common sayings is "Optics matter"—for the good, for the bad, for the generous, for the stingy.

One day my dad asked me to go on a run with him.

Halfway through the run, I asked him, "Where are we going?" He laughed and said, "Follow the rabbi." He was teaching me to trust the process. We ran up a huge hill, and at the top, he asked me to stop and look at what God has given to us to enjoy. As we started to walk down the hill, he said, "Hey, I have a quicker route. You want to take it?" Of course, I did, and we went straight down the hill weaving through bushes and trees. Once we made it out, I said I was going to take that route every time. So, now, every day I go on that same path and down that same shortcut. My point is, my dad is my guide. Who is your guide? Who are you guiding?

If your parents haven't been showing you the right path to take or setting an example of generosity for you, there may be other people around you whose habits you can copy. And, hopefully, you can share with your parents what you learn from others and from this book, and then you can start living the generous life together.

GETTING STARTED FOR GROWN-UPS

When my dad and I speak parents often ask me what they can do to get their kids to be generous. In fact, I am asked that question so often that I created an acronym: M.E.E. *Model, Encourage, Engage.* Using this formula will help you know where to start as a parent to get your whole family on board.

MODEL

For some people, modeling might be the hardest part. If you haven't been giving on your own, you're going to have to start; well, you *get* to start! Your kids need you to lead the way by example. But that means don't just write the check; live the lifestyle. Making your annual donation is fine, but if you really want your son or daughter to have the attitude of generosity, they need to see you putting these principles into action too. My hope is that you will make an effort to become aware of giving opportunities around you each day. Your kids will follow, because generosity is so contagious. It happened in my life because I started to follow in the steps of my parents. Those seeds of generosity were planted in my life because my parents were intentional about making it a habit.

ENCOURAGE

Encouraging your kids means two things: (1) motivating them and suggesting they practice giving—this may require you pointing out an opportunity and nudging them to make the right choice—and (2) supporting them in their efforts—meaning, when they see an opportunity, don't let your schedule or your mood keep them from following through.

Be sure you aren't forcing them; that will backfire. Present it as something they *get* to do—notice how I use the word "opportunity" a lot? Don't make it feel like something they *have* to do. Help them notice the people around them and the needs that might be there, and then point out how they might be able to make a difference. That will help them see the important role they can play in improving someone else's life. Who wouldn't want to be a part of that? Whenever I do something generous around my family, they always give encouragement and support to my idea. Be that encouragement for your kids.

ENGAGE

Engaging may be the most important component of all. Modeling the example is great and necessary, and encouraging your kids in their efforts will make it go further, but engaging with them and making it a family practice is the key for it becoming a lifestyle. Find giving opportunities to do together as a family. As you are developing a deeper relationship with kids, they will trust and imitate you. Just remember, it takes time. You won't get it right every time and your kids may resist initially. My parents don't get it right all the time, and they've been doing this with us for many years.

And one more thing: Be real. My parents admit their mistakes. They apologize. They ask for forgiveness. I know this has helped us have a real relationship. I believe it will for you too. Try sharing a recent giving story around the dinner table as a way to engage as a family.

WHERE IT LEADS

Even though M.E.E. is targeted to parents, it can be a great tool for all. When I started to be generous around my friends and modeled this practice for them, they caught the bug. We now encourage each other because we want to be supportive of one another. I had one friend who mocked it, but rather than letting him get me down, I decided I would be even more intentional with my generosity around him. I believe he will begin to see the importance of generous living as he sees the results of my choices.

We need to be bold—step out and be different—and I promise once you start, the people around you will join you. It takes only one person to start a revolution, and my friend John Maxwell said it so well: "A leader is one who knows the way, goes the way, and shows the way."[1] It starts with you, and you can't be worried about what others will say or think of you. Even if you feel like no one is realizing what you're doing, just remember that ILikeGiving.com started with no one noticing, but has now influenced over 100 million people!

Look for ways to start the generosity Ripple Effect in your family. (I'll explain more about the Ripple Effect in chapter 9.) Start by lifting your head and looking around for giving opportunities. I was at Costco recently, and as we were walking into the store, out of the corner of my eye, I saw an elderly woman. I smiled at her and then I noticed something. She was unable to get her groceries out of her cart and needed help. I ran right over to her and asked, "Hey, can I help you put your groceries in your car?" She said, "Yes, you are such a kind kid." As I was putting her groceries away, she said, "Thank you for looking out for people like me. I would have broken my back without you."

If I had been focused on my phone or thinking about what I was going to buy in the store, I could have missed that giving opportunity. Become more aware of your surroundings. Make the decision to look beyond yourself and your needs and look to the needs of others.

My simple story of helping an elderly woman is one way a person can start being generous. My sister, Gracie, is a perfect

---

1   Maxwell, John. *Quotes From John Maxwell (Life Wisdom Series)*. Nashville: Broadman & Holman, May 2014.

example of this because her school was helping orphans in Gulu, Uganda. She wanted to contribute, but rather than just getting money from our parents, she worked her tail off to raise the money on her own, and was able to give fifty dollars to the school fund. (That's like a million dollars for a fourth grader.) At that time she was saving up for a mermaid tail but decided to give her savings instead. The reason she wanted to give was because our parents planted seeds of generosity in her life and it seemed normal for her. What really made the difference between just making a donation and generosity being a lifestyle is that she also got to experience the joy of earning the money herself. That meant giving of herself instead of just passing along money from our parents.

I can only inspire and encourage you; I can't tell you where to give. Everyone has different giving experiences and opportunities. You might ask, where and how? Start by having an open mind and heart—move from being self-focused to others-focused. This will create a new way of thinking about the people around you.

Ethan is a good example. He was already doing something generous because he went out of his comfort zone to help people in a foreign country. While he was there, he saw another need—one he could meet—and he continued his acts of generosity even after returning home.

Accepting the Nudge to Give

ETHAN KING

At the age of nine, Ethan King went on a mission trip to Mozambique with his dad and came back with a bright idea. While he was in this foreign country, he had the chance to see how other kids lived, and he discovered what kids want in life really isn't all that different, no matter where you are. Ethan found kids his age playing soccer with balls made from garbage bag sand decided he wanted to provide them with the real thing so they could really enjoy the game.

When he got home, he started working on creating an organization called Charity Ball, which would give balls to kids who can't afford one. Then I Like Giving created a short film to show his generosity at such a young age to model to other kids. Ethan's story has been covered in countless articles and by news organizations, such as Fox and *Huffington Post*.

As he grew older, Ethan wanted to do more to help. In 2013, Charity Ball hosted a tournament with professional soccer players and three hundred kids. Ethan told me that it was a surreal moment to give those kids an opportunity that never would have happened if he had not stepped into generosity.

Other kids around the world who have been touched are working to help give soccer balls to those in need. The reason Ethan chose to give away soccer balls as his way of being generous was because his dad told him to use his gifts and passion to help others.

Ethan told me a story of a girl who wanted to use her gifts to help. This girl created her own jewelry and sold it to make money so she could turn around and give soccer balls to kids in need. When talking to Ethan, I asked him, "What impact has all of this had on your life?" He said, "It has been very humbling to give direction to this organization."

Thousands of balls have been given out in forty-seven countries because of Ethan's one decision to live a life of generosity. Ethan said that it all started with a mind-set of: *What difference can I make? I'm here on this earth for a reason, so how can I be generous with what I have?* As Ethan has said, "Giving has the potential to unlock [these kids'] future. This can open their mind to the future and forget what they have been through."

Today Ethan plays Division 1 soccer for Butler University and continues to pursue giving soccer balls away.

Ethan saw poverty and tragic circumstances when he went to Africa. There were kids raising their younger brothers and sisters because their parents had died. Their living conditions were unimaginable. Still, he noticed that they were kids and also loved to play, so he connected with them on that level and found a way to make a difference.

What you do in your life may not be as global as what Ethan did, but what you choose to do will still make a difference in someone's life. Ethan started where he saw a need and believed he had the ability to do something about it. That is how you can get started too. Just pay attention and make an effort.

UNDERSTANDING THE NUDGE

When you see an opportunity to give, you often feel something I call "the nudge." Let me break down what happens when you get the nudge. It may trigger your emotion to act upon your feelings.

My brother Dan has an incredible story of reacting to the nudge and acting upon it. One day, as Dan was rolling down our garbage cans to the curb—which was a quarter of a mile long—he noticed that our next-door neighbor who had recently broken his arm was struggling to balance and push two cans with one good arm. Dan quickly stepped in and said that he was not only going to help our neighbor that day but would also get his empty garbage cans back to his house once the garbage truck had picked up. The next week I observed Dan taking not only our garbage cans down but also our neighbors' cans. I asked him about it and he told me that he had told Mr. Bill that he would be happy to help him with not only the garbage cans, but also whatever else he needed help with while his arm was healing. I know that this surprised not only me but also our neighbor. Dan was a ten-year-old kid who saw a need, acted on it, and followed through on his commitment for weeks.

When you decide to take action, you may feel anxious. My sister, Gracie, describes it so well: "When I get the nudge to give, I get a rush of uncertainty and a sense of thankfulness for the opportunity God has given me." It isn't uncommon to have last-minute jitters or fears, though. The nudge can come in different ways for everyone, but you'll often hear a quiet voice telling you to act—it's your conscience telling you to give. It's like a tug on your heart. It might just be that you come face-to-face with a need someone else has, and no matter how you may try to ignore it, it keeps coming up in front of you. You know in your gut that it won't go away until you do something about it.

If you're reading this and thinking, *I haven't gotten the nudge in a long time,* it might be that you just aren't paying attention. When you make it a choice and become aware of your surroundings, giving opportunities will pop up everywhere. Get your radar working and that nudge will appear because you are opening your heart and looking outside your bubble. The nudge is part of becoming a generous person, but a nudge just helps move someone from the decision to the action of generosity. Don't wait for the nudge, because sometimes it won't happen. Once you have made generosity a habit—a way of life—you will often find you won't even have time to think or have a nudge because you will begin acting instinctively.

NUDGING MY DAD!

One day my dad and I went to the FedEx store and asked them to print off a couple of pages we needed. When we returned home we realized the pages were incorrectly printed. As we returned back to the store, we were faced with a choice: We could be aggravated about their messing up the order and take our frustration out on the clerk, or we could be gracious, explain the situation calmly, and ask them to reprint the order. We chose to be generous with our words.

As we were leaving, the kind lady helping us was walking out too. Walking to our car, I said to my dad, "Hey, let's ask her if she is going to lunch." When we asked, she said, "Yes." I said to my dad that we should buy her lunch, and then I gave her money. She was so amazed. Apparently, she had been short on money, and our generosity had changed not only her day, but also her week. She left with a huge smile and tears of joy streaming down her cheeks.

The whole drive home we had a meaningful talk about how we could have changed that lady's life with one decision to be generous. What if we had not stepped into that giving opportunity? We had no idea what that lady had going on in her life, yet we were able to step in and show grace and kindness. By doing that, I had a great moment to be generous in front of my dad to show how he has modeled generosity and activated it in me.

CHAPTER 4

Why Should I Be a Generous Receiver?

For my friend's sixteenth birthday, we went to play paintball. After getting all of our gear, we headed out for a three-on-three game. The first game started, and when I took my first shot, a paintball exploded inside my gun and I was unable to finish the game. I was so disappointed because I was going to have to sit out and watch my friends play.

As I walked off the field with my head down, a man approached me. "Is your gun broken?" he asked.

I nodded glumly.

He held out his gun to me and beckoned with his empty hand—he wanted to trade! When I looked at him in surprise, he said, "Well, what are you waiting for? Take my gun and get back in the game."

Hesitantly, I gave him the defective gun and took his gun. "Are you sure?" I asked.

"Of course! Have fun!" he said.

Excited to play, I ran out onto the field and began to shoot. As I was using the gun, I realized that his gun was better than what I had before. I ended up hitting everyone on the opposing team and winning the game for my squad. During the match, I noticed he and his friends cheering me on. After I handed the gun back to him, I said, "Thank you so much! That was the coolest gun ever."

He said, "You're welcome. I'm glad I could help your team win."

I gave him a high five, and my teammates were so happy that we had just won. As we were leaving the field, the referee ran over to me and said, "Dude, that gun you just played with is worth about four hundred dollars, and your first gun was worth around forty-nine dollars."

I was speechless. That man didn't even mention how valuable the gun was or warn me to be careful; he just said, "Have fun." That made me feel like a million bucks because he didn't care about himself and his gun; he just wanted us to be able to enjoy ourselves. It felt so amazing for someone to trust me with something they valued. His generosity meant I didn't have to miss out on playing with my friends.

What would have happened if I'd turned down his generous offer? Not only would I have missed out on a great time with my friends, but I would have hurt his feelings and taken away his joy in giving. Instead, receiving his gift with gratitude made me realize how much I wanted to be just like him, sharing my stuff and not being stingy about it.

WHY RECEIVING GRACIOUSLY IS SO IMPORTANT

You may not think how you receive has an effect on what kind of giver you are, but giving and receiving are so connected that you can't have one without the other. And, if you aren't doing one well, the odds are really good that the other one will keep you from being all you were created to be. It's like trying to ride a bike without wheels—giving is the bike and receiving is the wheels.

Receiving is an essential part of the giving experience, and receiving well starts with really understanding what receiving is all about. Many people have this big misconception that receiving means you are in need and that translates to weakness or being unable to provide for yourself. First, it's unrealistic to think we can get by in life without ever accepting help from anyone else. Even if we are in a position where we could buy whatever we want or need, we still depend on others to help us.

Matthew 10:8 says, "Freely you have received; freely give." This passage is so powerful in that we are asked as Christians to receive "freely" and do it well. We must understand that we need to receive because in the end we are accepting someone's generosity. Giving is a privilege and we get to be part of the greater good when we receive.

Think about it this way: You may have $50,000 to go buy a fancy new car, but unless you can manufacture that car by yourself too, that money is not going to get you what you need all by yourself. You have to depend on someone who has the skills to make a car for you, and you have to count on their generosity in being willing to share their skills.

Second, if everyone just wanted to be the giver and no one wanted to be a receiver, you'd have no one to give to, which would short-circuit the whole giving process. Like the guy with $50,000 has the money but not the ability to turn it into a car, the car manufacturer has the ability to make a car and needs someone to receive it.

I know you're probably thinking that the car example isn't very good because it is an even trade of money for goods or services. But think of the things you are able to do with your personal gifts and time; if no one wants to be a part of that or receive what you have to offer, it can make you feel really bad. What if you passed by someone who was struggling to carry a stack of boxes and you offered to help, even just to hold the door open, and they said, "I can do it myself!"? They are not receiving your generosity well, are they? Maybe they are suspicious of someone wanting to help. Maybe they think it makes them look weak. How does that make you feel? It may not make you unwilling to help the next person, but you might think twice about it because your offer was rejected.

Here's another example: At Christmas time, everyone gets really excited about giving gifts. Maybe you saved all year to buy something special for someone, and then you spent your time searching for that perfect gift. When Christmas Day finally arrived, you happily presented the gift and watched anxiously as that person opened it. You wanted to enjoy the look on your friend's face. What if that person opened it and said, "Oh, I don't need you to give me this," or "I'm sorry, I'm not accepting gifts this year"? You would probably feel really let down and hurt because you were denied the joy of giving. How would that impact your decision to give in the future? Would you be slow to give your next gift? It would be understandable if you were because you wouldn't want to experience being rejected.

IS IT REALLY BETTER TO GIVE THAN TO RECEIVE?

Everyone says it is better to give than to receive, and I have already explained why I think it is true for a life of generosity, but that statement is used mostly to speak to people who are doing more receiving than giving, in order to point out that there should be a balance. But if you are giving without ever receiving—whether you are just not letting others give to you or you just don't have people in your life who are being generous with you—that is also out of balance. I'm not suggesting you stop giving to correct this, but you may need to take a look at your attitude about receiving to see if you have the right perspective.

We are called to give without expecting anything in return. Yet God has put the principle of sowing and reaping into motion. There will be times in our lives when we give more than we receive, and times when we receive more than we give. A good example of this is the giving and receiving that happens between parents and children. When we are babies, it's all about receiving because we aren't capable of giving our parents anything other than the joy of getting to be parents, and even that isn't something we do consciously. As we get older, we begin to learn about giving and want to be a part of it. We enjoy getting to give our parents gifts on their birthdays or helping them around the house to contribute to the family. Still, they are carrying most of the weight in paying for all the necessities of life, driving us to all of our activities, and caring for us. It isn't until we are out on our own that they aren't doing most of the giving. That's when the balance shifts: We start taking care of our own children's needs, and when our parents are too old to care for themselves anymore, we might start helping them with things.

At least that's how it's supposed to work. And the only way it does is if we are willing to receive when we need help and give it when it is needed from us. It is better to give *and* to receive because that's what we were designed to do.

WHY WE STRUGGLE WITH RECEIVING

There are a number of triggers associated with receiving that cause us to shut down the giving-and-receiving process. We may think we are doing something good because we are not being greedy, not taking advantage of someone, or not being responsible for ourselves. The thing about generosity, however, is that you have to experience the receiving end of it to understand how much it means to be a part of the giving end. When you've experienced a time where someone did something for you and it changed your day or maybe your life, you realize what giving does for others and it makes you more willing to do that too. If you've never felt what it's like to receive kindness or help from someone, it is much harder to understand why it means so much to someone else. You can easily turn coldhearted, thinking, *I had to get here on my own, so they should have to do that too.* That is not a generous mindset. Let's look at some of the most common reasons people reject generosity from another person.

PRIDE
"I don't need your gift; I can do it for myself."

Pride is one of the most common reasons people reject someone's generosity. We work hard to get to the point where we can feel self-sufficient, and we take pride in that. It's okay to be proud of your accomplishments and the things you have done to improve your situation and get to a place where you can take care of yourself. But that becomes a problem when that attitude shifts into a mentality where you think you don't need anyone else. I don't think this is how we were created to live. We are supposed to rely on each other because we were made for relationship with others and with God.

I was in line with my friend at Chipotle one day when I noticed a businessman in front of me. After he handed the cashier his credit card to pay, they told him his card was declined. I jumped in and said, "I got it. I'll pay for his lunch."

The man said, "Are you sure? I have enough money; you didn't need to do that."

I told him, "Yes, I know. I want to be a blessing." I told him to have a great day and then went up to place my order.

When my friend and I sat down, the businessman came over and shook my hand. "You're a good man," he said. "You're so generous at such a young age. That is so amazing to see." He told me he would never forget this moment and couldn't wait to share it with his family.

My friend later asked if I thought that man would really remember that meal I bought for him. I said I was sure he would never forget it because it was probably the first time anyone had ever done anything like that for him.

Many people in that man's position might have refused

my generosity out of pride. Have you ever had an experience where your bank card was declined for some reason? I know how that can feel because one time I was buying some food and I forgot my wallet at home and I was totally embarrassed. Pride can really take over and cause you to reject the assistance you need. That man may have had plenty of money—maybe enough to buy everyone in the restaurant lunch—but, for whatever reason, he wasn't able to access that money at that moment and he needed help. When you have more than enough, it is easy to forget that not all needs are met with a full bank account.

I'm glad this man didn't allow pride to get in the way of accepting my generosity, because it made his day better, gave me a chance to do something nice for someone else, and caused my friend to become more curious about a giving lifestyle. Pride can prevent a lot of blessings and a lot of needs from being met. Don't let this mind-set stand in your way.

FALSE SENSE OF SELFLESSNESS

"I can't receive because you need it more than I do."

It is understandable that accepting gifts from some people might feel a little awkward if you know they are experiencing hard times, but it is important in living generously to be sure we are respecting others. Rejecting other people's generosity because you believe you are in a more stable position than they are might seem like a kind thing to do. It might feel like you are helping them out by not being a burden to them—but what you are forgetting when you do that is everyone needs to feel like they have something to contribute. It makes a big difference in people's outlooks on life when they feel they can do something to help others and brighten their day.

I was talking with a twenty-five-year-old man who told me that he does not like to receive gifts from other people who he thinks might have less than he does. He refuses to accept generosity from those he sees as being needier. Then he told me this story about a time when he was at McDonald's and the homeless man in front of him asked him what he was getting. The man said just a coffee. So, the homeless man decided to pay for the man's coffee. When he realized what had just happened, he totally denied and blocked this homeless man's generosity. The man said, "I can't take it!" The homeless man said, "Yes, you can. It is my chance to be kind and generous." The man turned him down and walked away.

When this man told me this story, I couldn't believe what I was hearing. I asked him, "Why can you be generous, but a homeless man can't? You may have totally stolen joy and happiness from this homeless man. How powerful it was that someone with so little decided to be generous with what he had. All you had to do was suck up your pride and take his generosity."

I tried to explain to him that everyone is a few decisions away from being in the same position as that homeless man. What the man didn't understand is that we all have pride and want to feel dignity. Pride can get in the way, but it can also be the thing that keeps us trying to improve our lives. For this homeless man, being able to do something nice for someone else gave him that kind of pride. And who knows? Maybe the homeless man had already received an abundance of generosity from someone else that day and he just wanted to pass it along. Maybe he was so grateful for what he had received that he wanted someone else to experience the same joy. We should never get in the way of people being led to give, because we don't know how that action will benefit them in the long run. Having the perspective that everyone is equally in need of self-esteem and respect opens your heart to giving *and* receiving.

PERCEIVED STRINGS ATTACHED
"You must want me to be obligated. No thanks!"

Sometimes we do need to discern the motivation behind a gift because there are people who don't have the best intentions. If you believe receiving a gift might put you into a bad situation, don't receive it. Trust your gut and pray for guidance and clarity. Most of the time, though, generosity does come from a good place, and those who are trying to give to you are doing it because they want to help, to be of service, or just to be nice.

One time, I started a conversation with the janitor at my school and told him thanks for all he does and that he was doing a splendid job keeping the school a clean place. He said, "Why are you so nice to me? No one ever thanks me for what I do. Do you want something from me?"

I told him, "Well, I noticed you and wanted to share that with you. I don't want anything; I just want you to know that

I have seen the countless hours you work to make this school clean and functional."

"You just made my day," he said. "You are the best part of my whole week."

I told him thanks again and walked away. It was great to know I could make someone's week just by using my words for good. Now in the hallways, I say hello and talk with him. He has gone from being a random person with a thankless job to a friend.

When you try to give to some people who are skeptical, they will ask, "What do you want from me?" I love this because I get to tell them that I want absolutely nothing! People on the receiving end of a giving experience often think they need to go out and give because someone gave to them. At times, when I give, I have to explain that I'm not expecting those people to pay it forward. I just want them to embrace my giving—just receive it. I believe that if I can get them to shift their attitude about receiving, they will eventually want to go out and give more on their own.

AN ATTITUDE OF GRATITUDE

If you are still struggling with receiving, try this: Be grateful. Sometimes what someone has to give—like the homeless man and the cup of coffee, or the widow and her mite in the Bible— may seem really small to me, but is huge to them because what they are giving is such a big percentage of what they actually have. Maybe they have plenty and can afford ten times what they are giving, but this is their first time giving, and they need to be encouraged in their change of heart. It could be that they are just filled with their own gratitude for what they have and want to share.

A friend of mine was blessed by the financial generosity of his peers. A simple act from his peers forever changed his life because they answered God's call, which was another person's prayer. My friend Austin has a wonderful story on how he was able to be the recipient of his roommate's generosity.

Receiving Well

Austin went to college knowing money would always be an issue and he would have to work his way through it the whole time. At the beginning of his junior year, he planned to be a resident assistant in his dorm, but he ran into financial obstacles and was going to come up short on his tuition, which meant he would have to drop out of school. His roommate decided to do what he could to help Austin come up with the $4,000 he would need, because he knew what an important role Austin played in the community of the campus. Austin told him not to do that because he didn't want to ask people for money. He didn't feel deserving of their help, but his friends wouldn't take no for an answer. Though Austin was in doubt that it would work, the money began flowing in, small amounts at first—pocket change, whatever a student had to spare—and then larger donations until they finally reached their goal just in time. His roommate didn't have any money of his own to spare, but he did see an opportunity to help bring together people who could. It changed the life of a friend and a community.

Remember, generosity isn't just about giving money. It is about kindness in our actions and words. It's about thinking about someone other than yourself. When you receive well—with gratitude—you may open doors to life-changing opportunities for other people. Austin had a hard time receiving, and that almost prevented him from being able to continue in college. Thankfully, he found his attitude of gratitude, and it made all the difference.

You don't always know why someone has chosen to give, or why that person chose you as the recipient. It really doesn't matter, because the reasons people give are personal to them. What does matter is that when you resist or reject receiving, this reveals your attitude toward gratitude. When you can have gratitude for whatever is given to you, the reasons you had for not wanting to receive just melt away.

CHAPTER 5
What's in It for Me?

One day my friend and I were at a fast-food restaurant and we passed an elderly man sitting alone. He seemed to be hungry and only able to afford a small amount to eat. We decided to buy him a gift card to help him out. We stood in line a little anxious but excited. When we got to the counter, we asked for a twenty-dollar gift card, on top of what we ordered for lunch.

The woman behind the counter asked us, "Why are you buying a gift card too?"

I told her we were buying it for an elderly man and were going to surprise him. I paid for the lunch and the gift card, she handed me my change and the card, and we left.

As I was walking away, I noticed that she had given me my twenty dollars back. Confused, I went back and told her she had given me back too much change. She said, "No, I didn't; I want to be part of this giving experience!"

It took me a minute to realize this lady had contributed her own money and wanted to be a part of this opportunity to be generous. So I thanked her, and then we went and gave the man the gift card and sat with him for a few minutes. We started talking and found out his wife had just passed and he was tight on money.

At the close of our conversation, the elderly man said, "I want to give all of you guys a hug, because you not only gave me a financial gift, but you also gave your time."

My friend's parents picked us up after lunch, and the first thing that came out of my friend's mouth was, "Mom and Dad, guess what we did today!"

Generosity can have a dramatic effect even if the person is only on the outside of the giving experience. I didn't expect the cashier to help with the gift card, but she wouldn't have received the blessing of giving if I'd been selfish and refused to let her participate, and then I would have missed out on my own blessing. If I had expected her to not charge me because I was doing something nice, I would have cheated myself out of the benefit of giving, because I was doing it for the wrong reasons. When people give out of duty and compulsion, they lose the benefits and joy of giving.

I know it may seem strange to ask, "What's in it for me?" in a conversation about generosity, especially after the example I just shared; but, if we are being honest, this is something that often comes to mind. This isn't necessarily a selfish thing. It's normal to ask why you should do something when you're faced with making a sacrifice of some kind.

What I have found is that living generously is how I was created to live—how we all have been created to live. When I'm not living a generous life, I'm not functioning in the way I was created, and things start to break down mentally, physically, and spiritually in my world. Generosity is something we all desperately need in our lives, but we often don't understand how much we need it. When we live how we were created to be, we live the best life possible.

There has been a lot of research done to study the effects of giving on our lives, and they have found that there are mental, physical, and spiritual benefits to giving. So, let me tell you how generosity actually does benefit you.

MENTAL BENEFITS

The University of Notre Dame spent $5 million doing a study on the human brain and discovered two main things: first, we are designed to give; second, the brain needs to be actively giving.[2] (In other words, none of this is once-and-done stuff!)

When we give, our brains produce oxytocin—a powerful hormone that is linked to empathy and generosity—and it produces a feeling of connection. This makes all the sense in the world to me. It supports my belief that I was created for relationship with God and relationship with man. Oxytocin has been proven to provide a sense of inner peace, making givers more tolerant and relaxed. Based on this information, you can see how oxytocin is a stress-busting benefit to giving.

Think about the generous people you know. I bet you will find they tend to be happy, fun, and a touch more chilled out! When you add in the effect of dopamine—it plays the euphoric role for the giver—you have a one-two punch of positive sensations that the brain associates with generosity. So, with two feel-good hormones being released when you give, why wouldn't you want to do it often and make it a part of your daily life?

_____

2   /http://generosityresearch.nd.edu

The effect on the way we think and feel is probably one of the more obvious ways giving benefits us. My dad has always said, "I can honestly say I have never met an angry, bitter generous person," and I totally agree with that. Givers are joyful and positive in their outlook.

The dictionary defines generous as: "1. liberal in giving or sharing; unselfish; 2. free from meanness or smallness of mind or character; magnanimous."[3] When we think of giving, I believe most of us focus on the first part of that definition and see it as a selfless act—as something that has to be good for someone else and that doesn't do anything for us; however, the *International Journal of Behavioral Medicine* reports that generosity is actually in our best interests, stating, "Altruistic...emotions and behaviors are associated with greater well-being, health, and longevity." In other words, giving doesn't have to hurt to be effective.[4]

The second part of the definition is "being free from meanness." Think about that for a minute. How hard is it to be mean when you're joyful? In *I Like Giving,* my dad explained a lot of the science behind what happens to us when we give. I think it's pretty cool that we are made in such a way that when we do something good for others something happens in our brains that makes us want to repeat that action.

In 2017, a huge review of forty studies on volunteering's effect on general health and happiness was published in the journal *BMC Public Health.* The results? Volunteering not only

---

3   http://www.dictionary.com/browse/generous
4   https://link.springer.com/article/10.1207%2F-s15327558ijbm1202_4

improves well-being and life satisfaction, it's also linked with decreased depression and a lower risk of dying early. "Since people reporting stronger social relationships have a reduced risk of mortality, the social aspects of volunteering may contribute to the observed survival differences," the researchers wrote in the review. "Taken together, this review suggests that bio-social and cultural factors may influence both a willingness to engage in volunteering, as well as the benefits that might accrue."[5]

According to a 2012 *Psychological Science* study, people get more psychological benefit out of giving than they do receiving.[6] Think about the times you've given of yourself. Now think of the times you've been on the receiving end of things. Of course, it's better to remember when someone helped you or did something nice for you.

The thing we forget, though, is that to have a sustained impact on us as the givers, generosity has to become a way of life. Nearly everyone feels the need to give during Thanksgiving and Christmas, but in January the giving oftentimes slows way down.

One of my first experiences with giving was in sixth grade when I bought ice cream for the kid in front of me in the school lunch line because he didn't have enough money. It may not sound like a big deal, but it was the beginning of my generosity journey. My friends saw this and asked what a lot of people ask: "Why did you do that? You don't have to."

---

5   https://bmcpublichealth.biomedcentral.com/arti-
cles/10.1186/s12889-017-4561-8

6   https://www.huffingtonpost.com/2012/08/16/feel-more-giv-
ing-receiving-generous-generosity_n_1776839.html

I was happy to explain, "I know I don't have to; I don't have to do anything. I get to do this."

That day, I couldn't stop thinking about the next giving opportunity I would have. It totally changed my thought life because I wasn't thinking about Drew, Drew, Drew, anymore. I was now thinking about others! That change in me never would have happened if my parents hadn't planted those seeds and modeled a giving lifestyle. The feeling you get from giving can actually be as addictive as a drug, but in a good way. Give it a try and see how your thought life changes.

When I discovered that teenage suicide is greatly reduced when people bring generosity into their lives, I was taken aback! Teen suicide is at a crisis level in America, and here is a very practical, non-medical solution to solve a societal problem that is affecting hundreds of thousands of teens each year. I'm not suggesting you can replace the care of a doctor for any mental health needs you have, but there is obviously a mental shift that happens when you focus on someone else and stop worrying so much about the things that are troubling you.

One of the easiest ways to start giving is by being aware and attuned to the needs of others around us. I have always looked out for the kids in school who struggle to make friends or have a disability. On my first day of high school, I encountered Tim. Through the weeks, I noticed him struggling with school and with making new friends. Tim has terrible vision and is very short. I made it my mission to acknowledge him in the hallways in order to try to become friends with him.

After a while, whenever he saw me, his face would light up, and with a huge smile, he would say, "Drew, how's your day?" I would take a minute to talk with him and find out how he was doing. The best part is I am usually with other friends, so they get to see the time I'm taking to talk with him. Those friends of mine now say hi and talk with him as well.

That first day of school, I made one decision to reach out to someone who needed a friend, who needed to be acknowledged. We all long for connection and to feel noticed and valued. By incorporating generosity into your life, you will find yourself reaching out to the people around you and making those connections that make a difference in your life and theirs.

Who is the Tim in your life? The next time you run into yours, just take a moment to speak to them and improve their day. It will have the same impact on yours.

PHYSICAL BENEFITS

Have you ever seen the glow on a giver's face? It comes from the joy, anticipation, and happiness that come from giving. And that's nothing compared to what you see on the face of the person receiving. The effects generosity has on us physically are significant. In *Why Good Things Happen to Good People,* Stephen Post explains how the research he did shows that we live longer, take less medicine, and have better relationships when we live generously.

Researchers have been doing studies for years in an attempt to demonstrate the physical and mental benefits of giving, and they've consistently found that giving makes people feel good. They have seen that it doesn't matter if generosity is in the form of volunteering or donating money; a selfless action can help reduce the risk and symptoms of depression and everyday stress.

The *American Journal of Public Health* published a study in 2013 that found when people give their time and assistance to others, it reduces stress, which is a risk factor for many chronic diseases. The study followed nearly 850 adults in the Detroit area. Though stress did not predict mortality for participants who had helped others within the previous year, researchers did find a link between stress and mortality in people who didn't lend a helping hand, even after taking age, health, and other factors into consideration.

But the most important thing these studies found about giving of time or money was that the key component of it has to be heartfelt. Your intentions, or how you feel about the action, matter when it comes to giving. "If it's a meaningful donation, it can have a significant impact," Stephen G. Post, director of the Center for Medical Humanities, Compassionate Care, and Bioethics at New York's Stony Brook University, said. "But if it's trivial or just grudging or whatever, probably not."[7]

The reason this is true is that meaningful giving takes the focus off yourself and your everyday stresses. You can write a check to a charity and it probably isn't going to have the same impact because you aren't really thinking much about where the money is going and the difference it will make. But when you give part of yourself in an unselfish way, the difference is noticeable. Post explained, "People say their friendships are deeper, they're sleeping better, and they're able to handle life's

---

[7]   Renter, Elizabeth. "What Generosity Does To Your Brain and Life Expectancy." US News and World Report. https://health. usnews.com/health-news/health-wellness/articles/2015/05/01/ what-generosity-does-to-your-brain-and-life-expectancy (retrieved October 16, 2018).

obstacles better. . . . And the amazing thing is, you don't need to go to a drugstore for it."

Another study followed over two thousand residents of Marin County, California, and found that the mortality rate for those who volunteered regularly was lower than those who exercised four times a week, as well as those who attended church regularly. Those who "volunteered for two or more causes had a 63 percent lower rate of mortality than people who didn't volunteer during the study period."[8]

Philippe Tobler, associate professor of neuroeconomics and social neuroscience, who also conducted a study on generosity, said, "It is worth keeping in mind that even little things have a beneficial effect—like bringing coffee to one's office mates in the morning." And according to the study, other research suggests that making generosity a habit could have an impact on your long-term well-being and happiness.[9]

The motto at I Like Giving is "We believe a generous world is a better world for all of us." My dad always says giving is a heart issue. Of course, he's not referring to the physical heart but to our emotional heart. However, the things that affect our emotions have been proven to have an impact on the health of our physical heart as well.

---

8   https://health.usnews.com/health-news/health-wellness/
articles/2015/05/01/what-generosity-does-to-your-brain-and-life-
expectancy
9   http://time.com/4857777/generosity-happiness-brain/

SPIRITUAL BENEFITS

There are many spiritual benefits to living generously. Let's take a look at them through the lens of the here and now, as well as the lens of eternity. I have found in living generously that I experience joy, happiness, better relationships, and an overall great life. I have bad days (who doesn't?), but they seem to be not as bad as they could be, and the recovery seems to be quicker now that I have stopped living just for me. In my day-to-day life, I see myself looking to others instead of thinking about myself. My friends have observed my generosity, and they are beginning to apply the same practice to their own lives. I have seen a change in how they talk and act toward their teachers, classmates, and parents. The effects I've been describing in this chapter and that I've experienced in my own life are the "here and now" earthly benefits.

When I think of how these earthly benefits are impacting my life and the lives of others, it makes me realize how closely they are connected to heavenly benefits as well. Christians are called to be like Jesus, and being a generous person is one step closer to being like him. I often say I am most like Jesus when I give. I know that sounds a little prideful, but I can't think of anything else that would rank higher on the scale of things that are Christlike. I bet you're thinking, *What about forgiveness, Drew? Isn't that one of the main things Jesus teaches?* My answer would be that forgiving others is being generous!

Jesus talked a lot about money in the Bible because it is a powerful test of our character. It is a picture of what we value. Jesus said that where your treasure is, there your heart will be also. The implication is that if you look at where you invest, spend, or give your money, you will find that is where your true love lies.

I would encourage you to think on that and then figure out if where your money is currently going really reflects what you believe as a Christian you should value most. It might be that you need to adjust your priorities, or it might just be that you need to shift your practice to model what you preach. If you spend most of your allowance or the paycheck you get from your part-time job on video games, and aren't setting aside any for saving or giving, you know your priorities are out of balance. If you are setting most of it aside for a car when you get your license, and you won't chip in to help your family buy a nice birthday gift for your grandma, you probably aren't living generously. I have always cared about others, but I didn't always use what I am blessed with to help others. After I started living generously, the way I wanted to spend the money I earned changed.

The Bible is full of promises about generosity and future rewards. In the book of Matthew, Jesus said to "store up for yourselves treasure in heaven" (Matthew 6:20). In other words, do things and live in a way that allows you to increase your heavenly savings account! Jesus said if you give even a cup of cold water in his name, you will not lose your reward. God says that if you trust him and give generously, he will bless you! He wants us to give of ourselves because he has equipped us with everything we need to do that. When you really grasp that you were created by the most generous God, and you were created to live this way, you will begin to enjoy giving.

My friend Caroline Brewster has learned the joy of giving in a really unique way. In searching for a solution to her own problem, she is giving hope to future generations.

Finding True Generosity
Caroline

My name is Caroline Brewster, and I am sixteen years old. On December 1, 2008, when I was seven years old, I was diagnosed with type 1 diabetes (T1D). All I understood at that point was that it would take a lot of hard work, involve a lot of restrictions, and there's no cure. It was a burden I would have to carry for the rest of my life.

What I didn't realize at the time is that I could live a successful and normal life with this disease. With the right tools, I could continue to eat whatever my heart desired, participate in and love sports, school, and extracurriculars, just the same as I did before; however, I could never take a break from the rigid requirements for managing my disease. *Ever.* Sometimes I asked myself, "Why should I continue to manage something so closely if there's no light at the end of the tunnel?" But that all changed when I met my best friend, Katherine Hellmers.

Our moms met at a Juvenile Diabetes Research Foundation (JDRF) meeting. I had met a lot of kids with T1D and I thought they were all pretty weird, so I wasn't expecting anything different with Katherine. We finally met, and to my surprise, we hit it off immediately. Katherine is hilarious, kind, and relatable in every aspect of life. T1D bonded us closer, since I can relate and connect with her over the struggles of T1D. We both desperately want a cure, and sitting on the sidelines, waiting for a cure, was not an option. We *had* to make a difference in the T1D community for the other million Americans and their families that fight the tough battle every day.

At just nine years old, we came up with the idea to start a campaign to raise money for the JDRF, but we didn't want to go with the classic lemonade stand. We wanted the idea to be something new, unique, and professional—in other words, legit. All the money would go toward research for a cure through the JDRF.

The Christmas season was coming up quickly and we were thinking of what we might sell. It had to be something that went along with the holiday season. We decided mistletoe would be fun and festive, so we began selling mistletoe to "Kiss T1D Goodbye" as the YuleT1De girls. We sold professional-looking packages of mistletoe at the JDRF Holiday Luncheon for $10 a bag. We got all dressed up and spoke in front of a huge crowd, pitching our "Kiss T1D Goodbye" idea and mission. By the end of the afternoon, we had raised about $500!

After that, we were so motivated to keep raising more money. We want to see a cure in our lifetime so the generations after us don't have to deal with T1D. But since you can't sell mistletoe year-round, we decided to sell chocolate Hershey's Kisses at other JDRF events to "Kiss T1D Goodbye" all year.

Our next huge event was the JDRF Dream Gala, where we offered bags of Kisses for a $1,000 fund-a-cure donation. After we poured our hearts out on that stage, bid cards flew up by the second. At the end of the night, we received $40,000 in donations. Katherine and I were ecstatic, knowing that all this money from these generous donors would go toward curing this disease.

Since then, we have continued to fundraise at more JDRF Holiday Luncheons, Dream Galas, and other events. As time progressed, we got more and more comfortable speaking about our story and raising awareness. We graduated from selling our little bags of Kisses to selling personally branded "Kiss T1D Goodbye" lip balm. Over the course of six years, with the help of many very generous JDRF supporters and hard work, we have raised a grand total of almost $200,000 to support research for a cure.

It is humbling to know that we have contributed to a brighter future for people like us. Katherine and I want to escape the shackles of this disease, and so do another million Americans and their families. Through this, I've learned that trials and hardships are part of God's plan and happen for a reason. It's all about how we react that makes us learn from our situations. I have learned my purpose in life: to glorify God with the gifts he has given me. No matter what you've got, give and serve for the glory of God. If God opens the door to opportunity, walk right in and use it. Be the hands and feet of Jesus Christ.

Type 1 diabetes has helped me discover my love for service and being a voice for others. Raising money and awareness fills me up, knowing that the money raised goes to research for the betterment of not only me and my best friend, but for all the other type 1 diabetics. So, yes, I don't like giving. I *love* giving. Giving gives me a sense of community and so much joy, love, support, and motivation all along the way. Giving gives me hope.

So, you can see from Caroline's story that her acts of generosity have not only benefited others; they have also given her life purpose.

MOTIVATIONS

There are three main reasons I am motivated to live generously, and they are what keep me in a lifestyle of giving even when I face obstacles or disappointments. First, the reaction of the person receiving is worth it all. In every giving story I've shared so far, the expressions on the faces of the people who received were priceless and unforgettable.

Second, there is this thing I've mentioned before called "the giver's glow." It's the physical, emotional, and mental feeling that you experience with giving. You start to notice yourself feeling a little lighter—maybe you even catch yourself skipping or jumping, but definitely smiling a lot more—because of all the joy you feel. Your thoughts are changed because you can't stop thinking about what just happened. You can't help looking forward to the next time you're going to be generous. This is when the oxytocin has overtaken your body and you feel so great inside.

Finally, the thought that you're making the world a little better is a really incredible thing. In a time when hate seems to be everywhere, the love that is spread by generosity gives me hope for humanity. We all want to make a change in the world, and sometimes the size and scope of the problems we see can feel really overwhelming. We have to remember it isn't our job to fix them all, but if each of us does one small thing each day to improve the way we treat those around us, little by little, it will make a difference.

RIGHT MOTIVES

Having the right motives is an important part of living generously because it is what takes giving from being a charitable action to a lifestyle. Sure, if you give a hundred dollars to the Red Cross when they do a donation drive, it will help people. But if you add to that the gift of donating blood regularly, volunteering to help with community education programs, or going with a disaster relief group to an area affected by a tornado or a hurricane, you are giving in other meaningful ways. When I think of good motives, several things come to mind—it helps others; it makes me feel good; it makes the world a better place.

Anytime we are seeking to have a positive impact, we are working from right motives. But, for me, another motive is obedience. God has instructed us to be generous with one another, and it's not just one of those "Because I said so" instructions, like you get from your parents. It's because he knows all the ways giving benefits us and he sees how the Ripple Effect of our giving will change the lives of people we haven't even met. (I'll explain more about the Ripple Effect in chapter 9.) If you could see ahead of time the difference your generosity would make in someone's life, wouldn't that motivate you to give even more? Well, even though we can't see into the future, God can, and we can trust that if he is leading us to act generously with someone, it's because there is a good reason for it.

WRONG MOTIVES

Maybe you have heard the biblical saying, "Do not let your left hand know what your right hand is doing" (Matthew 6:3). That may sound a little confusing, but basically what it means is that when we do the things that God instructs us to do, such as giving, we should do a heart check. Our motive for sharing needs to be pure. If we are looking for our reward and approval from men rather than from God, we have missed the mark.

I do believe that most acts of generosity will end up working out for good, but there are times when our motives can get in the way of it having the full impact it could have, and it definitely can affect whether or not we receive any benefit. When you are choosing to be generous, ask yourself, "What do I expect to get out of this? How will I feel if I don't get that outcome?" If your answer is you-focused, you may need to think about whether you have the right motives.

OBSERVATIONS AND OUTCOMES

1. *Generosity brings freedom.*

One of the greatest benefits of giving is freedom. We free ourselves from thinking we are better than someone else. We may gain freedom from all the misconceptions we hold about giving. And that frees us up to give. So many people are enslaved by their day-to-day lives and don't look outside of themselves. Giving will free you from being selfish and self-centered and will help you become others-focused.

When we give, we feel freedom from judgment from our peers. I started to become the person I was made to be because I didn't care about what my friends thought. If your friends stop talking to you because you start living generously, they aren't your friends. Some of my friends aren't generous because they are fearful of the outcome and response. I tell those friends to become bold and remember it's not about them.

2. *Generosity creates joyfulness.*

When I speak about giving at conferences, donor gatherings, and churches, I have so many people come up to me with the giver's glow and they can't wait to tell me their giving story. I love to listen and be a part of these stories, but it brings mixed feelings for me when I discover their story is from twenty years ago. It's amazing to me that someone can still be so joyful over a story from so long ago, but it's a bummer that they haven't had that experience since then.

What if we could have this giver's glow every day of our lives? Generosity will turn you upside down and flip the switch of joy. When Jesus spoke of the man who found the treasure in the field, he emphasized how "in his joy" the man went and sold all that he had to gain the treasure (Matthew 13:44). We're not supposed to feel sorry for the man because it cost him everything. Rather, we're supposed to imitate him. It cost him, yes, but it gained him everything he wanted! It filled him with joy. The benefits vastly outweighed the costs.

3. *Generosity fuels generosity.*

Generosity is contagious. Don't believe me? Just try it and you'll see! I have seen how my friends have caught on to the joy that I get from giving, and they are now doing it too. They want to be a part of what happens when you brighten someone's day with a smile, a kind word, a helping hand, or an unexpected gift. I've also seen the people I've been generous with turn around and do something nice for someone else. It really does feed on itself in a good way.

CHAPTER 6

Do I Have to Be Generous?

"No, of course not" is the obvious answer to the question "Do I have to be generous?" No one has to give anything to anyone, do something helpful for anyone, or show kindness. But what kind of world would that create for us? I certainly wouldn't want to live there. Would you?

So, why should you want to be generous? I covered several benefits in the previous chapter that are a pretty good motivation for giving. But, in case you need more, we're going to talk about some of the benefits to others and the world around us.

I think the reason living generously is not automatic for everyone is that we each bring past experiences to the idea of giving that affect our attitudes about it. Some people never had generosity modeled by their parents, some tried to give and something happened to make it go wrong, and some give for the wrong reasons. In this chapter, we are going to look at some of the things that can stand in the way of giving and how to get past them. I have different categories of givers and nongivers that cover most of the perspectives people have about giving. You may see yourself in one of these. If you do, pay close attention to the suggestions for how to change your attitude and find the joy in giving that I know is there.

GIVERS: THE GOOD, THE BAD, AND THE INDIFFERENT

The reason I am so passionate about generosity is because I am made in God's image and He is the greatest giver of all. It makes me sad to see the negative effects of not giving in our lives, because I know that is not how we were created to live. I see people who avoid generosity or don't do it consistently, and I know that if they understood what true generosity is, they would embrace it as a lifestyle. So, let's take a look at the different types of givers/nongivers I've identified as I've observed people.

THE SELF-PROTECTING

First, there is the person who has been abused by generosity in some sort of way. Maybe a gift was used in a way it wasn't intended, or it could be that someone scammed them. Those are tough experiences to go through and can be a big roadblock. We are going to talk more about messy giving—what happens when giving goes wrong—in chapter 8, but it is important to understand that this is one of the areas in life where things get better if you keep trying.

Another way people are wounded from generosity is when someone refuses their attempt to give. This could mean they use what I call "killer phrases," which are huge roadblocks to people, especially if it's their first time giving. Some examples of killer phrases are: "You don't have to" or "Are you sure you want to do that?" While these don't seem harsh, they can totally disrupt someone's giving. People often respond in this way because they mistakenly think they are being generous themselves since they aren't taking a handout. These types of rejections discourage the giver who doesn't want to be unappreciated, and it tells the receiver that accepting help makes you weak.

I have talked with people who have told me their first giving experience was very awkward because the person didn't receive well, and they stopped giving as a result of it. One time, I told one of my classmates that he had a great memory for details. The guy turned around and said, "Why are you being so nice? Are you trying to get something from me?" His response was very unexpected because I was just trying to be generous with my words. I asked him to simply receive my compliment as encouragement without any ulterior motive. We need to not jump so quickly to negative conclusions. I believe he responded the way he did because at some point in the past someone may have used flattery to manipulate or use him and now he is overly cautious.

It is a real bummer when the way people have been treated in the past affects their ability to receive kindness in the future. Being suspicious of someone's generosity is a sure way to stop the "Ripple Effect" in its tracks. (More on that in chapter 9.) But if you run into a block, and feel yourself wanting to stop trying to be generous, it is time to ask yourself why you were giving in the first place.

Was it to feel good about yourself, to get praise or recognition, to get something in return? Or was it to meet a need you saw in someone else, to brighten someone's day, to show someone how generosity changes lives? If the outcome of your giving isn't what you expected, perhaps you had the wrong expectations.

Getting over this kind of block starts with a change of intention—remember it's not about you; it's about them. It takes commitment and courage to step outside your personal bubble and do something for someone else. When you do this, what you reap is better than the fear you had to overcome in the first place.

THE SELFISH

The second type that resists giving are people who actually are selfish and don't want to give up what they have in order to help someone else. Many people are selfish because a person, thing, or place has affected them in a negative way. Many people can judge and assume that these people will never change.

I disagree because everyone can make the decision to change and move toward generosity. This doesn't mean the first time you do something generous for someone else, you become selfless. You need to make it a habit and work at changing your lifestyle—shifting your thoughts, words, and actions. Your thoughts are affected by past experiences, so start new with a fresh perspective and think positively about the people around you.

How you use your words with the people you interact with also reflects whether you are selfish or selfless. I remember a very shy kid in my class and how hurt he was because everyone made cruel comments about his weight. Not only is that kind of bullying and teasing unnecessary, it's destructive. It is usually done to make the people saying these things feel better about themselves. That's one of the most selfish behaviors

I know of. Selfless people look for ways to be uplifting, positive, and encouraging.

Remember, actions speak louder than words, and the way we interact with one another is a huge part of generosity. The simple way to overcome this obstacle is to take a minute and put yourself in the other person's shoes. If you see homeless people on the street, instead of criticizing them for how bad they smell or what a bother they are, imagine what it would be like if your parents lost their jobs and couldn't pay for the house anymore and you had to live in your car or on the street. How would you want people to treat you? If that's too much of a stretch, just think about if someone stole your wallet and you didn't have money for lunch anymore. What would you hope someone would do for you? It's really easy to stop being selfish. All you have to do is think about someone else's need above your own.

THE SELF-CENTERED

Possibly even more concerning than people who resist giving are those I call self-centered givers. These are people who decide to give, but are self-focused, making sure their wants and desires are met first. They either skimp on what they agree to give, make you feel bad about what you need, or hold it against you and keep an account of how much they've given. They may give, but their attitude will steal any possible joy from it.

I have a friend who is a self-centered giver and it's tough to see. There was a time we decided to go in together on a present for another friend for his birthday. The shirt cost fifty dollars and he asked me to buy it and said he would pay for his half later. I bought the shirt, wrapped it, and we gave it to our friend. After I asked my friend about reimbursing me for his half, he said he would send it when he could. Two months later, nothing had been sent; I didn't want to be rude, but I asked again. There was no response. The next time we hung out, he told me he was sorry, but he didn't have the money. It was so disappointing to see my buddy be so stingy. The worst part was that he had bought a new electric skateboard the day before. I wasn't upset about the money but about the fact that he had totally lost the right perspective on giving. It seemed that giving became more of an expense and obligation than a joy.

Self-centeredness is harder to get over because it comes from an attitude of the heart. Sometimes it is motivated by selfishness—just not wanting to give up your stuff—but it can also come from a feeling of lack. The fear of not having enough can cause people to hold on tightly to everything they have. When we lose sight of why we are giving, we become an obligated giver—someone who just writes the check or treats it like a bill they have to pay. There are a lot of emotions you have to deal with around this behavior, but it helps if you start with baby steps and first give something that you don't need. See how that feels and realize that you are going to be okay without it. Next time, you can give a little more. Maybe you don't get your Starbucks latte so you have the money to buy someone who is hungry a sandwich instead. And then you just build from there. I think you'll find that the fear you have around not having what you need is unrealistic and that you end up having more than you need in the long run. Sometimes that's because you realize you don't need as much as you thought, and other times it's because you are blessed by other people's acts of generosity to make up the difference.

THE SELF-SERVING

Self-serving people want to use generosity as a way to boost themselves up higher and make them look "good" to the people around them. It's easy to recognize self-serving givers because either they make sure everyone sees them being generous or they only give if they will get something out of it. Maybe it's celebrities who show up to a charity event with a bunch of paparazzi to make sure they get media coverage or someone who only donates money for the tax deduction. It might also be people who do volunteer work just to make themselves look good for their college applications.

There have been times in my life when I felt God was giving me the nudge *not* to tell a giving story. Even though I think it's a perfect idea, God can close the door. Giving has boundaries. I need to remind myself every day that all generosity opportunities could be an assignment from God. God is using us to answer someone's prayer. So, when thinking about it that way, I find it's hard to mix it up.

I took a mission trip during my freshman year of high school, and after returning, I wanted to share pictures on social media. The truth is, my intentions weren't entirely pure. I was being driven by self-serving motives. I wanted people to see that

I was doing good things in this world. It was kind of like, "Oh, look at me!" As I was about to post it, I felt the Lord say, *No, let's not do that.* I knew there was nothing inherently wrong with what I was doing, but I wasn't doing it for His glory; I was doing it for myself. I wanted people to see me, me, me. I had the message all mixed up.

There may be a time when you might feel God saying don't talk about that giving experience. This book is full of inspiring giving experiences, and they are meant to motivate you to try living generously yourself. But there have also been some stories I wanted to put in this book that I, ultimately, felt were supposed to remain between God and me.

If you find yourself having a self-serving attitude about giving, you have to shift your mind-set from seeing generosity as a means to an end or as something you do to help yourself. That may not be easy at first, but with some intention, you can do it. If you have been giving to impress people, try doing something generous without telling anyone and see how long you can keep it a secret. It's kind of fun to watch someone be filled with joy from a surprise gift and wonder where it came from; in the meantime, you are the only one who knows the truth about it, while others are guessing.

Also, it's okay to take a tax write-off for your charitable giving. I'm not going to criticize you for that, but if you only do it at the end of the year when you realize you don't have enough deductions, you are missing out on so much. Give throughout the year, anytime you see a need. It will help you catch the giving bug, as it becomes more of a habit.

THE SELF-ABSORBED

Self-absorbed people aren't necessarily selfish or greedy. They usually are just wrapped up in their own world and not paying attention to the people around them. They may choose to be generous, if they stop thinking about themselves long enough to see the needs around them. They might even be really generous in what they give or how they help someone, as long as it doesn't affect what they want for themselves.

Let me confess something to you: I still don't get this generosity lifestyle perfect. There are times I just walk past a giving opportunity right in front of me. One time, I went to a driving range to hit golf balls with a couple of buddies. As we carried the bucket of balls to the range, I noticed a kid out of the corner of my eye who had dropped all of his balls on the ground. What did I do? Nothing. I kept going, acting like I didn't see him. I felt the nudge to help him, but I just kept walking because I was in such a hurry to go do my own thing. I could have helped this kid out and modeled generosity right there in front of my friends, but I chose to focus on my own needs.

As you begin adopting the lifestyle of generosity, it can be easy to beat yourself up for missed opportunities. I do look back on that day and wish I'd done better, but it is not useful to feel guilty about it. I am human and I make mistakes, and sometimes I just totally miss. The important thing about these types of situations is that it makes us more aware. I use it as motivation to make sure I jump on the next opportunity that comes my way!

If you find yourself experiencing this block of self-absorption, one of the fastest ways out of it is to think about something you need right now and if you need someone's help with it. Now think about how you would feel if that person didn't come through and help you, and you were left to deal with this on your own. That's an uncomfortable feeling, isn't it? When I thought about the fact that I'd actually been in the other kid's position before and how bad it made me feel, I really felt bad about not helping him. I think even the most self-absorbed people will be able to shift their thinking to consider the needs of others a little more when they put themselves in the other people's shoes.

THE SELFLESS

Selfless givers are the people who don't let excuses get in the way of giving opportunities. They think about how others' lives will be changed when they give of their time, abilities, or other resources. They aren't concerned with what they can get out of a giving opportunity, though they understand their lives will be improved. When you are selfless in your generosity, you look for giving opportunities instead of waiting around for one to drop in your lap. It becomes a lifestyle where generosity is second nature and you don't even have to think about it.

ORGAN DONORS

Holly was a typical teenage girl who was active in school sports and other activities until the day her liver failed without warning. She ended up in the hospital with her health going downhill fast.

Within eight hours, Holly received a transplant that saved her life. She then began the long road of recovery back to being the athlete she once was.

She had the opportunity to participate in the Transplant Games—Olympic-style events for people who have had organ transplants—and so she began training. Holly wondered how she could ever thank someone for the gift of life she received. She decided if she could draw attention to the difference being an organ donor can make, it might save other lives.

A few years later, Holly received a letter from her donor's mother, Helen, and she had an opportunity to meet her and thank her for her son's generosity in being willing to donate his organs. She gave Helen the medal she won at the Transplant Games to show her appreciation for the life she was given and to share with her the victory that came from her son's generosity.

Being an organ donor is an extreme example of what it means to be a selfless giver. If we can all make an effort to do something for someone else that isn't driven by a need to feel good about ourselves, the desire for attention, or the appeal of having something to put on our college applications, the benefits reach so much further. And all it takes is thinking beyond our own needs for just a minute.

MAKING THE CHOICE

As I watched my parents model generosity for our family, I had some questions. I'd see my dad do things like buy iced tea for the dry-cleaning employees because it was one hundred degrees that day. At first, I wondered why he would spend time and money to do something like that. Then it dawned on me that he has made generosity such a part of his everyday life that being a blessing to others is just a habit—he doesn't even have to think about it anymore. As I watched more and more of my parents' generosity, I finally figured out why they do it.

First, I see what a difference it makes in their outlook on life to be able to put themselves in someone else's shoes and make a difference in their lives. Becoming others-focused changes their attitude and how they approach life. They find it easier to manage their own problems when they remember that other people have needs and obstacles to overcome as well.

Also, I have seen a change in how they talk. Instead of complaining about how long a line is, they comment on what a great job the employees are doing in managing the busy time. They are more joyful and peaceful. My dad has said, "When we give, we think we are changing others' lives, but really we are changing our own hearts."

The last reason I think my parents live generously is they see the effect it has on people. My parents haven't just modeled generosity to me; they are modeling it to all the people who witness their generosity—the employees, the other customers, their friends, their colleagues. They become swept up in what I call the "Ripple Effect" (more to come on that in chapter 9), and it becomes contagious. The first giving we did as a family was replacing the stolen bikes for a father and son in our community, which I shared in chapter 2. That one simple story turned into ILikeGiving.com, which has inspired over 100 million people to begin living more generously.

Experiencing the impact my parents' generosity has had on them and those who receive from them made me want to start being different and living the fruitful lifestyle of giving. We all have choices in life. We make hundreds of decisions in a day. Why not let the simple choice to live generously be one of them? It will take commitment, but it starts with a subtle shift in how you live, and it will change the outcome for you and the people around you forever.

One time, I was in a sporting-goods store looking for a special kind of ball. I was having a tough time finding it, so I asked someone. I waited in the sporting goods department for ten minutes for someone to help me. When an employee finally approached me, I had a decision to make. I could either make a big scene and complain about how bad the customer service was, or I could give him the benefit of the doubt that he was not ignoring me but was instead helping other people or fulfilling another task for his job.

I chose the generous approach. He helped me find everything I needed and more. We ended up having a great conversation, and then he rang me up. He thanked me for being so kind and patient. He even gave me a 20 percent discount! If I had taken a confrontational attitude with him, I probably wouldn't have received as much help as I did, and I definitely wouldn't have had an enjoyable time shopping. In this case my gracious attitude resulted in him being generous with me.

Because I had been generous in my attitude with him, he was then generous with me.

My ability to handle that situation is a direct result of the generosity my parents have modeled for me. I have seen my parents in similar situations in the past. My parents encourage us to show generosity to the people we interact with. All children learn from their parents' behavior, and as we get older, we learn from the behavior of our peers. Making the choice to model generosity for those around you is an important first step in changing the hearts and minds of everyone you meet.

The question of this chapter is "Do I Have to Be Generous?" As we have demonstrated, you don't have to be. However, after seeing how easy it is to improve your life and the lives of those around you, why wouldn't you?

CHAPTER 7

What Do I Really Have to Give at My Age?

When you are young, it is quite common to wonder what it is that you have to give. I have asked it a lot myself. Watching my parents give to the people they interact with, I would sometimes wonder why they were so kind and generous with everyone. At times, I was even suspicious of why they did it, but over time I wanted to know how I could be generous too, even as a kid. I've been fortunate to have parents who modeled this way of life for me. Many of my peers haven't even thought about what generosity is because no one has been teaching them about it; this saddens me. I do believe that if more people started living a little more generously, it could change the world. I will get into this further in chapter 9 when we discuss the Ripple Effect.

Whether you are young or old, it is easy to get caught up in focusing on your limitations. You could be thinking, *I am totally broke. How can I be generous?* In this book, I am speaking to young people—kids, teens, college students—who mostly don't have their own financial resources yet. As you go into retirement and have to live on a fixed income, this question of "What do I have to give at my age?" will come up again. Though this chapter will be mostly written for my peers, I'd encourage you to look back at the story of Evelyn ("I Like Being 98," shared in chapter 2 as well as in my dad's book *I Like Giving*), who was still doing for others when she was nearly one hundred years old.

I'm not going to go through a list of things you have to give at your age because they are going to be unique to your situation and your personal gifts and talents. What I am going to do is give you some steps to follow that will help you figure out what you can give and how to find giving opportunities.

GET CURIOUS

One of the first steps is to ask questions. By asking, "What do I have to give at my age?" you are on the right track. The next question to ask is, "Who can I give to?" You can start by looking outside yourself and your friend group to become aware of who is around you. One way to be generous is to lift your head up from your phone and pay attention. It means thinking about someone other than yourself. Get curious about what else and who else is around you. There is an amazing world of people and opportunities for you to do something that makes everyone's life better one gift at a time.

During my sixth-grade year, I saw a kid sitting by himself and told my friends we should go sit with him. From that day forward, he sat with us, enjoying conversation and friendship. Our new friend, Alex, had special needs and one of the biggest hearts ever. One day, Alex told me he was going to a special-needs carnival and wanted us to come with him so he didn't feel alone. I gathered my friends and we went to the carnival with him and had a blast. He had the best time of his life and it meant so much to him to have us there. He gave me a hug, and his parents told me afterward that he couldn't even sleep the night before because he was so excited he had friends who actually cared about him. Then they told me he had been bullied before he came to our school.

After that, I became intentional in including him in our group. Every year, we attended the carnival with Alex, and more people in the school wanted to go because they looked beyond his differences and saw him as the awesome person that he is instead of some weird person with a disability. My one decision to be curious and step outside my bubble changed my life and the lives of a lot of kids in my school. Acceptance and kindness are among the many ways we can be generous at a very young age. Being curious about others, instead of being judgmental, is a great way to give something that can make a huge difference and cost you nothing.

PAY ATTENTION

The next thing that happens after we get curious about others is that we start paying attention to their needs. We are able to see ourselves in their shoes and have empathy for them. That means we start to understand what they might be feeling and want to help them improve their day. It means standing up and standing by people you see with a need. It means having the courage to make the choice to be generous, instead of ignoring a need when you see it.

Bullying is a problem in our culture today, and a lot of attention is being drawn to it. However, it's not enough to point out bullying when it happens; we have to stand up for others when we see it. I've seen lots of bullying in school, and I make sure to call people out when they are being negative or mean to someone, making fun of them or pushing them around. Standing up means if the kids with disabilities in your school are being teased, you become their friend and show others that they are a human being and deserve respect. Standing up for others, instead of putting them down, is one of the best acts of generosity you can display, and you can do it at any age, no matter what your circumstances are.

TRY IT

When you give for the first time, you might feel many different emotions. You might be anxious or nervous about how the person will respond to your generosity. I can guarantee that you won't ever know until you try. And I can suspect that most of the time it's going to go better than you imagined.

When I started noticing the people around me and seeing their needs, I couldn't wait to give. Once you do it the first time, there are more and more opportunities that will come your way. It reminds me of the first time I did something nice for another person on my own. I bought an ice-cream cone for the kid in front of me in the lunch line. It felt so good that I kept wanting to do more.

Once you have started getting curious and have taken the step of standing up for another person's needs, all that's left is to do something about that nudge. I know that can be the hardest part. If you are still unsure about what you have to give, then try giving your time to someone or saying a kind word.

My friend Denis found an everyday problem but created an everyday solution. Oftentimes the best gift you can give someone is friendship and relationship—the simple idea of looking to the needs of the people around us.

"WE DINE TOGETHER"

To some, it may not seem like a big deal, but lunchtime for a young person at school can be one of the hardest periods of the day if you have to sit alone. Sitting by yourself might be a welcome time of peace and quiet for some, but if you are new to a school or feel like you don't fit in, that part of the day highlights how alone you feel.

Denis Estimon is a student in Boca Raton, Florida, who started a club called "We Dine Together" to make sure no one at his school ever had to have that experience. He felt that same loneliness when he first came to the United States from Haiti and didn't know anyone at school. As a senior and a popular student, he was in a position to make sure others could have someone to eat lunch with and take an interest in them. His club has changed many lives and is expanding to other schools around the country.

His simple act of generosity with his time and attention has had a huge impact on his community. As it grows, it will have the potential to address the biggest problem driving students to depression, violence, and suicide—the need to feel seen and heard and valued. Denis probably didn't have any idea that his choice to sit at lunch with someone who looked lonely could have grown into this, but this is what living a life of generosity does.

BE AN EXAMPLE

One of the best parts of starting to live generously is that people will observe your behavior and start to wonder why you are doing what you're doing. They are going to get curious too. That means you've triggered the steps toward a life of generosity in them. They may not have anyone else around them modeling giving, so you could be the only example they will see.

One day I was out with some friends and saw a police officer. I went up to him and thanked him for serving and creating a safe environment for our community. My friends were shocked. After I shook his hand and walked away, my friends asked, "Why did you do that?" Honestly, I hadn't given it much thought, but I realized that my parents had modeled respect for those who serve. It had just become part of my everyday life. That day, I was able to model respect and generosity for the police officer to all of my friends. I told them that using my time, influence, and words are great ways to be generous.

It is important for us, even as kids/teens, to notice and give recognition to the many people who are not always appreciated. The reason I took thirty seconds to thank the police officer was because I already had made the decision to live the habit of generosity in my life. It had simply become second nature to me.

After that day, one of my friends approached me at school, totally serious, and asked, "What is generosity?" It was a great opportunity for me to explain what generosity means to me. There may have been more people in my group of friends who didn't know any more about generosity than he did; he was just the one who had the courage to ask what it meant. Because of that, I had a chance not only to explain what giving is and how to do it, but to help him understand why I continue to give. If everyone started living generously through their words, actions, insights, influence, personal belongings, and money, the world would be a better place.

We know that so much of the hatred in this world comes from not having empathy for other people—not seeing the other person's side of things, not being able to put ourselves in someone else's shoes—and from being self-focused. Generosity changes us spiritually, mentally, emotionally, and even physically. It changes our attitudes toward ourselves and toward others; it changes our desire to do things that aren't just for our own benefit, but for the greater good.

DON'T WAIT

So, what are you waiting for? Are you feeling the nudge? Are you starting to notice that there are things you can do to make a difference, or at least wishing there were? If you wait for your parents to start modeling generosity to you, that might never happen. You actually might have to model it for them, especially if they didn't have anyone setting the example for them as they were growing up. Think about it: If you wanted to play a sport, like football, would you just sit back and wait for the ball to fall into your hands? That's not how it works, and in the meantime, you aren't getting any closer to doing what you want to do. If you have a crush on someone and you just sit back and wait for that person to read your mind, what's going to happen? Nothing. You may miss out on a chance to know someone special because you are waiting. So, start for yourself.

I understand that you may not have money to give, but that is only one way to be generous. If, as kids and teens, we just say, "Oh, we're too young to give," we are stealing joy from not only ourselves but also others around us. If you wait for the perfect giving opportunity to come knocking on your door, it's likely not going to happen. Giving might be messy, denied, awkward, confusing, unexpected, or amazing. When you decide to give hope, you will release your expectations of giving going the way you think it should go. This is a good time for you to check your motive on giving. If you only give to look good to your parents, teachers, peers, college applications, and social media, I would encourage you to change your motivation. It will never work because giving starts with your heart. If you're doing it for the wrong intentions, the impact might not be the same.

If we continue to use age as an excuse in our giving, our inactions can have a negative impact on others' lives. Those opportunities may disappear as someone else will come along and provide for the need, which will result in a missed opportunity for true joy.

A WORD FOR PARENTS

If you are a parent reading this book and looking for ways to help your kids be more generous, that will make me really happy. This is a great start for leading them to becoming who they were created to be. Here are a few things that I have learned as a sixteen-year-old about how to inspire and motivate your kids to give. I have put together a list of dos and don'ts that will help.

Dos:
- Define generosity for your family.
- Talk with your kids about what giving means to you and for your family.
- Work with them to come up with a few ways to give as a family.
- Check your own motives for why you want your kids to give.
- Create opportunities for them to choose to give.
- Encourage them and support them when they come to you with a giving opportunity.

Don'ts:
- Never force them into giving.
- Don't make them feel guilty if they don't want to be generous.
- Don't forget that this is not about you; it's about them growing as people and helping others.
- Never discourage them from following a nudge and seizing an opportunity for generosity.
- Don't let them give up if giving goes wrong.

You are their greatest support as they try to adopt a lifestyle of generosity, and the best thing you can do is to decide right now to join them and make these changes in your own attitudes and behaviors. Make the choice to grow together in generosity.

CHAPTER 8

What If Giving Goes Wrong?

By now, you may feel inspired to give this generosity thing a try. Maybe you still have concerns and are asking, "What if giving goes wrong? What if I have a bad experience?" Well, I can pretty much guarantee that at some point your giving might go wrong. But it's okay! Giving doesn't always go the way you think it will go. There might be rejection, abuse, or ingratitude, and those things are not fun to experience. You don't have to let them affect your future giving and steal your joy. Remember, when you give, you should always keep the attitude that whatever happens, it is not about what you want to get out of it; it is about what you want to do for others. It is important to push through those early feelings of being awkward, disappointed, and intimidated. You will discover a better life and a better you! The good definitely outweighs the bad if you just keep trying.

WHEN GIVING GOES WRONG

The ability to forget a gift gone wrong and move on shows a generous person's true colors. There will be times your generosity is going to be received poorly. Maybe they will take advantage of your generosity or misuse your gift. It could be that they will just be ungrateful or won't acknowledge it at all. Any of these things could affect the outcome and the way you feel about giving in the future. In this chapter, I want to help you see past those disappointments so you can keep giving and discover the joy that it brings.

REJECTION

One of the most disappointing giving experiences you can have is when someone rejects your generosity. You've decided you want to share something with someone; maybe you've put a lot of thought into what kind of action you want to take and are really excited about the opportunity . . . and then this person tells you he doesn't want what you are offering. He could just say, "No thanks," and move on, or he could be mean and criticize you or what you were giving. It's a real letdown in a time when you had been feeling really good. I wouldn't blame you a bit if you thought, *That's it. I'm done trying.* But I don't want you to stop there: Don't let that person keep you from the joy that comes from giving. Don't allow that experience to prevent someone else who will receive well from getting the benefit of your generosity.

Once, I was riding a bus to a sporting event and it was very full. An elderly lady was standing near me while I was sitting. I asked her if she wanted to have my seat. She glared at me and, with a huge attitude, said, "You think I need to sit, kid?" This totally threw me for a loop and I didn't know what to say. I finally said to the lady, "No, I just wanted to be generous with my seat." She looked at me with disgust. I was so confused. I was expecting her to say thank you and accept my offer. I never imagined she would take it as an offense. I don't know what had happened in her life that made her react that way. I could have let this affect my willingness to make a kind gesture like this in the future, but I knew that was her issue and the next person might really appreciate being able to sit down.

Thinking about the possibility of making someone's load a little lighter, and how it made me feel, is something I want to keep experiencing. I know that what I wanted to do was a good thing, and that was something I wanted to keep experiencing. I am glad I did not let that experience hold me back, because I have had so many other times when people were really grateful. They have told me that what I did changed their lives. That makes the risk of rejection worth it every time.

ABUSE

It's sad to think that someone would take advantage of your generosity, but it happens. Those people are not only hurting you, they are hurting other people who need your generosity too. Ultimately they are hurting themselves, because that kind of sin in their lives keeps them from receiving real blessings. They won't ever be truly happy with the things they take from people who are trying to be generous. Most of the time, these are not the types of people you will be helping when you choose to give. There are many more people who are legitimately in need, and who will do the right thing with what you offer them, so don't let this fear keep you from giving.

My dad made me aware of a time when someone took advantage of his generosity. A man was once in need of clothing for his job. My dad decided he would take the man to a store and allow him to shop for some clothing. My dad told him to pick out whatever he wanted, but not to go over a certain limit. The man agreed and began picking out items. When he was finished, they went to the cash register and everything he selected came out to be just at the limit my dad set. As Dad was about to pay, the man ran to get a couple more things. The items he brought back to the counter took the total way over the limit. My dad didn't want to make a scene, so he bought all the stuff, but he felt his generosity was being totally abused. He told me he felt gross inside because he was trying to be generous and this man pushed him into being an obligated giver. He felt really taken advantage of in this experience. For a few weeks he didn't give, fearing the situation might happen again. But, my dad told me, he decided that one selfish man wasn't going to steal joy from his life, so he forgave the man, moved on, and didn't let one person's actions prevent other people from being helped.

I wish I could guarantee that your good intentions will always be rewarded with positive experiences that bless everyone involved—but giving involves people, and people aren't perfect. What I can guarantee is that you won't regret trying again. I've given you suggestions for how to feel out a situation to determine if someone might abuse your generosity, and those tips can give you confidence to keep trying. But they won't always help you avoid people who will use your gift inappropriately.

INGRATITUDE

There will be times when the response to your generosity that you were expecting never comes. You will probably give many times expecting at least a thank-you from the person, and maybe a smile, handshake, or hug. After all, it's normal to expect people to show some sort of gratitude when you do something nice for them. But not everyone knows how to receive generosity well, as we discussed in chapter 4. If you go into your generosity lifestyle expecting that everyone is going to pat you on the back, tell you what a great person you are, and sing your praises to everyone they meet, you are not only going to be disappointed, you are doing it for the wrong reasons.

Gracie's story is a great example of how it feels when your generosity is not acknowledged. This was her first attempt at giving on her own, and it did not go as she expected.

GRACIE'S Giving Situation

Gracie ran into her brother's room one day with an overwhelming surge of joy. She announced that she had discovered the best giving opportunity that just couldn't be passed up. She went on to explain that her math teacher had run out of dry-erase markers for doing math problems on the whiteboard. She said she wanted to give him a new set of markers and an eraser.

That night, her parents took her to the store to pick out the gift. She wrapped the gift and decided she wanted to surprise him by slipping the markers on his desk with a copy of the book *I Like Giving.*

All day, her family was so anxious to hear how her giving experience went. When she came home from school, she reported that something bad happened—the teacher already had new markers in his desk. She said she felt so stupid for giving him something he already had. The math teacher didn't even acknowledge the gift, which made her feel worse.

That night, she said she had expected some kind of gratitude from him, but the opposite happened. Gracie had seen her family give many times and receive thanks from those they helped, so she had an expectation of how people may respond. When it didn't go that way, she was really disappointed and struggled with her feelings. Thankfully, because her family had been modeling generosity to her for most of her life, she was able to try again and has had many positive experiences since.

You may encounter people who respond to your generosity with ingratitude. Other times, they show their ingratitude by simply taking what you are giving and not acknowledging it. You *cannot* let those reactions make you bitter or ungrateful. Instead, smile, move on to the next giving opportunity, and enjoy making a difference for someone who will really benefit from your efforts. Even though you didn't get the response you were expecting, you may have changed that person's day and attitude for the better. You don't always get to see the outcome of your generosity.

HOW TO RECOVER

If you get upset at the person or decide you're never going to give again, that doesn't help anyone. Be proactive rather than reactive. In fact, one of the best things you can do after a bad giving experience is to go right out and find an opportunity to have a good one. My brother always says, "If you fall off the horse, you get up and keep going." If someone takes advantage of your generosity, forgive that person and move on. If you offer your seat to someone on the bus and they react with resentment, offer it to someone else. If someone takes more than you were planning to give, try to recognize the ways that you are blessed— at least my dad had enough money to cover what this guy bought and we were still okay. The right perspective helps a lot. Don't bring an old, negative situation into the next potentially good one. See each new opportunity as a fresh start with a chance to make a difference.

Here are some tips for how to approach giving and to shift your perspective if things go wrong.

MANAGE YOUR EXPECTATIONS

It is important to go into every giving opportunity with an open heart, but also keep your mind open with no expectations. This will make your giving experiences even better. I try to remember that giving isn't about me. It's about my being obedient in responding to the nudge to do something for someone else. With that as your focus, you can be happy you gave, whether the other person received well or not.

LET IT GO

Don't let a bad experience ruin your day or even stop you from giving. Laugh it off and keep giving. Treat it as a learning opportunity. Maybe you discovered through the experience how to better assess risks and handle those situations. You can also learn to have sympathy for others. People don't react to kindness with anger unless they have been hurt in some way in the past, which has affected their ability to trust. Pray for them and hope that they can learn to accept generosity in the future. And who knows? Maybe your attempt at giving is what begins to change their attitude. Regardless, move on and look forward to the next opportunity!

DON'T GIVE UP

Giving up is not an option. People who give up are quitters. You can't live a happy, joyful, and fruitful life without embracing generosity. It's so hard for me to imagine my life without giving. Giving is a part of me; it's addictive and fun. I remember the time in my life when I stopped giving, and I remember feeling something was missing. Something was taken from me that brought me such joy. I had a negative attitude and was selfish. Even though the reason I had stopped giving was because of a disappointment, I felt even worse from not being generous than I did from the giving gone wrong. When I realized that, I said I would never stop giving again.

My dad loves to ask, what if giving goes wrong? Actually, the question should be, *when* giving goes wrong, how will you handle it? If the generous life were depicted on a graph, you sure wouldn't see a straight line moving steadily up and to the right. We have setbacks, dashed expectations, disappointing encounters, and deceiving receivers. Sometimes when giving goes wrong, it is on the giver. Sometimes it's on the receiver. Sometimes both.

I clearly recall a time our family was at Chick-fil-A at the UCI campus in Irvine, California. We had recently moved to California and were so excited to be sitting outside enjoying lunch. As soon as we lifted our heads from thanking the Lord for the food, an unkempt lady appeared with a small child. She had the classic small cardboard sign in her hands as she leaned into our table.

She asked for money or any help for her and the child. It was very uncomfortable, like when someone gets in your personal space and you get a whiff of his or her breath. The table went silent. My dad felt paralyzed. Then he moved into solution mode—not generosity mode. He reached into his pocket and pulled out twenty dollars and handed it to her.

As she slipped away, no one said anything. Several minutes ticked by before he broke the silence. "So, who wants to say the 'Giving Guy' just missed on that one?" I was the first to jump in. The giving felt forced. It felt pressured. I asked my dad why he gave money to her. He shared how she made him feel guilty, like she wasn't going to leave without giving to her. Her attitude and actions that practically forced my dad to give to her bugged me the rest of the day.

A day earlier, I had been at a printing store with my dad. As we returned to pick up our order, we noticed the lady who helped us heading to her car. We both sensed the idea to give her ten dollars for lunch. She loved it. She said we made her day. She made ours.

Within twenty-four hours, we went from having a great giving experience to the opposite. Sometimes giving goes wrong. You may be wondering if the Chick-fil-A experience put a damper on my giving. That's a fair question. It easily could have left me a bit jaded and added another layer to some of the unhealthy thoughts I have had about people with signs. However, I caught myself. I found myself being grateful that I wasn't in her situation. I quickly grabbed hold of the reality that if I stop giving because of giving going wrong, I would be robbing joy from so many other giving opportunities that come my way daily, weekly, monthly.

Giving will go wrong at times; it can't be avoided. If you stop giving, the odds are 100 percent that you will only have bad giving experiences. If you keep trying, you will find that you have more good experiences than bad ones. Remember, no one is a perfect giver and no one is a perfect receiver, which means there is never going to be a perfect giving experience.

Every giving experience is different; be optimistic and remember that if your motivations are good, the outcome doesn't matter. And, keep in mind, you often won't know the final outcome of a giving opportunity. What may seem to you like it went wrong could be the start of something going really right in that person's life later on.

CHAPTER 9

What Is the Ripple Effect?

One of the best things about giving is the Ripple Effect. The generosity Ripple Effect is the wave that potentially never ends on each act. The reality is you may never know just how far-reaching your act of generosity goes.

For example, the first time we gave as a family, as mentioned already, was when we heard about a father and son in our community whose bikes had been stolen. When we decided to help them, that one story launched an organization called I Like Giving, and what we have done by sharing other people's giving stories has inspired millions of people around the world. People today are looking for a way to change the impact they have on the world; they want to build better lives and better futures for their families. It is a pretty big goal to try to reach around the world and make a difference, but it is doable if you remember the impact of the Ripple Effect. Let's start right at the center and work our way outward and look at the lasting impact generosity can have.

IMPACT ON YOURSELF

In order for the Ripple Effect to reach your relationships, your community, and the world, it has to start with you. Before an attitude of generosity can touch others' lives, it has to touch yours first. Over time, this way of living will weave itself into your inner thought process, and eventually you will be giving without hesitating. It will become a habit—a really good one.

It may seem contradictory to focus on yourself when talking about generosity, but that is where it starts. Sometimes people need a little personal motivation for giving. They may need to see a benefit for themselves before they can look past their own needs to help others. We covered the ways giving benefits us in chapter 5 and it's not just a self-serving thing. It's even okay that we keep giving because we get the benefit of feeling good when we do it. It keeps us giving to others, and that's what matters. As I began living generously, I thought I was doing something good because I was changing other people's lives. What I didn't realize until later is that these daily choices to look for ways to give to others has ended up changing *me* as a person. Instead of focusing on how busy my life is, I have started to look outside myself. I have integrated kindness and generosity into my everyday life, and it makes me happier and it drives me to want to spread that joy to those I come in contact with each day.

One day, I was sitting at a restaurant working on homework and I noticed something. I saw a woman cleaning the tables, picking up trash, and making the place clean for the next customers. Her cart was perfectly organized and she clearly took pride in what she did. I began to wonder what I could do to make her day better, since she put so much effort into making a difference for others through her job. I decided to thank her for her hard work and to buy a ten-dollar gift card for her.

After I got the gift card, I walked over and told her, "You have such a great attitude, which I admire, and you do such a great job every time I see you!" I gave her the gift card and instantly I could see her spirits were lifted. She gave me a hug and said, "Thank you!" She couldn't stop smiling at me, and I was so happy that I had been bold enough to be generous toward her.

At my age, making an effort to be generous and respectful to everyone has really changed how I see people. Everyone is equal, and I want to treat people that way. The reason I even thought of buying her a gift was because my mind-set has changed from being all about me, and now I intentionally lift my head up from my phone so I can notice opportunities like these. This has changed my actions, and my goal is to approach every day being as selfless as possible. It's not about being prideful but mindful.

IMPACT ON YOUR RELATIONSHIPS

The people close to you—your friends, family, classmates, teachers, neighbors, etc.—take notice of how you live your life. If they are already living generously, they can be a great support system for you in your giving. You can develop a special bond around your giving experiences and deepen your relationship. When I witnessed my parents giving, it made me curious. That prompted conversations about why they did what they did. As we have begun giving as a family, we have begun to talk and be more real with one another. I have noticed a shift in my words, and how I honor and show respect to my parents. Of course, there are still times I get frustrated or mad at them for some reason. But the way I am now able to respond in those tough times has strengthened our relationship.

I believe that by bringing generosity into your relationships a bond happens. Whenever a team wins a championship, they have a strong bond with each other. I believe that same thing happens when generosity happens together. My dad is one person in my life with whom the bond has become super strong. It started with him modeling to me at such a young age.

It reminds me of the first time our family decided to give together. My dad was reading the newspaper (who reads that anymore?) and found a story of a family who had their bikes stolen. The bikes were the child's toy and the dad's way of transportation to work. He said to us kids, "What should we do?" At seven years old, I said, "I can give my blanket." Obviously, that was no help, but the thought was what counted. Then my brother said that we need to go buy them bikes! So, our family jumped into the car and drove to the bike store. Once the bikes were in the car, we stopped at the first stop sign and my mom looked over to my dad and asked, "Do you know their address?" He looked at her and said, "Shoot, they didn't put the address in the newspaper." So, after four hours of driving around our town, we finally found them. Because of the language barrier, all the son and dad could say is "I like bike" as they rode down the sidewalk. My brother and I agreed that was so much more fun than going to the water park, which we were planning to do that day.

That was a monumental moment in our family because it started a culture of generosity in our family. This bonded our family and brought us closer together. We continued to do more and more giving experiences as a family. The reason I brought up my family's first giving experience is to remind you that this is how my story began. I am part of the Ripple Effect too.

I have people come up to me after I speak and share their giving story from over twenty-five years ago. Do you know why they still remember and tell their story from so long ago? I think it's because they're going back to one of their first giving experiences that shaped their outlook on the generous life.

Think about the power of one decision and the effect it can have in your family, on your sports team, or in your group of friends. Each person has the opportunity to touch the lives of many people in their sphere of influence. Instead of being negative and hurtful, choose to be positive and loving. You will probably encounter some resistance at first with some people who aren't used to generosity. Just give it time and change will happen.

Remember, generosity changes your heart and makes you treat people differently. We could stop the brokenness and anger that leads to bullying, abuse, and neglect because people would be concerned for one another rather than seeing them as enemies.

IMPACT ON YOUR COMMUNITY

Your community is looking for a change, and it could start with you. We have seen a lot of division lately, and most people don't want to live that way. They are looking for a solution to be able to get along better with the people around them. They want a better quality of life for everyone. I will let you in on a secret: If you decide to make a difference, you can. Whether you are at the farmers' market, a soccer game, school, or church, how you choose to interact with the people in your community is key.

One day as I was leaving golf practice, I saw gardeners doing a great job working on the landscaping. I thought, *If that was me, I'd be hungry.* Then a thought came into my mind: *What if I go to Krispy Kreme and buy them some doughnuts?* So, I went and bought a dozen and was really excited to give them these doughnuts. As I was heading back toward the gardeners, I got a hunger pang and ate one of those doughnuts. When I finally arrived, I gave them the eleven remaining doughnuts. I told them thank you so much for the hard work they do, day in and day out. I wanted to give them some doughnuts as an encouragement and acknowledgment of their work. And as I left, I said, "These are some really good doughnuts!" Pulling out of the parking lot, I looked back and saw their faces with pure happiness. They received well!

Look for places that need help, and be the helping hand. This might be serving the homeless, working on a project to build a home for a low-income family, cleaning up a park for neighborhood kids to have a safe place to play, or any number of ways to better your community. When communities come together to do good, great things happen because of the Ripple Effect. And sometimes it's through something as simple as being a pleasant person to be around. Instead of honking for the old woman walking across the parking lot to get out of your way, go help her with her groceries. If you see someone being bullied, don't laugh or turn your back; say something, stand up for that person. Let someone go ahead of you in the checkout line if he has fewer things in his basket. Start living and breathing generosity, and others will too.

When you model generosity, others take notice because you are different in a good way; you will stand out (until we get everyone on board with the generosity lifestyle). You can't expect change from others unless you have changed yourself. Shift your thoughts, your words, and your actions toward others. This will launch you in the right direction toward generosity. Don't be afraid to flip the switch to giving. It's a huge step in creating a community of love and joy.

IMPACT ON YOUR WORLD

The world is a really big place, and it's hard for anyone to imagine having an impact that could affect so many people. It's next to impossible for young people to think they could make a difference. We see lots of negative and hurtful news stories all the time. It can be very discouraging to see people who are older and seem smarter and more powerful than us struggle to figure out how to get along and do what's right. This is when the question "What do I really have to give at my age?" can really stop your generosity in its tracks. But what if all it took was a little generosity carried forward by the Ripple Effect? What if your kindness, your desire to give and make someone else's life better, actually could change the world? Well, I think you'll see by James Dennehy's story that you are never too young to start working to change your world.

JAMES DENNEHY

James Dennehy is part of a family full of adopted children from many different countries, many with significant physical disabilities. James is originally from India and was born with no arms. James's family's story was featured in the "I Like Adoption" video that you can watch at ILikeGiving. com.

Even with his disability, James was just like most kids his age, headed to college and looking forward to exciting things in his future. But one day, he got a call. The 2012 video about his family had been widely viewed by members of the Obama administration. Many in the White House loved the film and wanted James to come work with them. When James got the phone call from the White House asking him to come to Washington, D.C., for the summer and be an intern, he was shocked. An internship was definitely not part of his plans, but he gladly accepted. James ended up working in the Office of Public Engagement and Intergovernmental Affairs.

James told the *Daily Press* that the hardest part was having to wear a tie, but he figured out that tying it before putting it around his neck helped. As the summer went on, he was able to learn how to tie it while it was already around his neck. What an incredible way to adjust to challenges! Because of the video about James's family and the follow-up interviews done on him after his internship, a lot more attention has been brought to the need for adoption of children with disabilities. Hundreds of people around the world have adopted children because of their story.

I truly believe if everyone decided to live a little more generously every day that the world would be a different place. It can start with how we talk and act toward someone—a simple compliment or a thank-you can go a long way. Maybe you will be called to serve an area in need. If everyone could experience, even once, the real joy of giving, I believe they would never turn back. When giving becomes a habit, you will start to give your money without thinking you're losing it. You will only think about the good it is doing.

The I Like Giving films have been viewed over 100 million times around the world. They connect with the messages because we were born to be generous. Giving will unlock the heart of anyone because it brings out something special that's already inside. Many people say they want to change the world; most don't realize that the change can happen with something as simple as a little generosity. The Ripple Effect will take one small action all the way around the world.

IMPACT ON ALL GENERATIONS

Probably the most important impact of the Ripple Effect is the one that carries on for generations. It's the most lasting and far-reaching influence we can have—to change the way future generations think about generosity and approach giving. What if, instead of being known as "tech necks" or iGen, the self-absorbed generation that is too attached to their smartphones, we came to be known as the Generous Generation? What if we began modeling generosity in new and profound ways for the generations that preceded us and those that will follow? We have so many opportunities and so many resources available to us, and we will be influencing the next generation in one way or another.

What impact do you want to have? We can use our technology, our knowledge, and our potential to bring the world closer to us. We can change it for the better, not make it smaller, where we don't see beyond our screens. By influencing our generation and the next (and the next), we can reverse the effects of selfishness and hate. It starts with me. It starts with you. It starts with us.

ACKNOWLEDGMENTS

I want to give thanks for the skills and talents that God has given to me to be able to help others. I want to thank my mom and my dad for investing in me and believing in me. My brother Dan and my sister Gracie have both been huge supporters in making this book happen.

I am so grateful to have such an amazing book team. Cara Highsmith, Mitch Shea, and Kevin Harvey have helped glue the pieces of the book together. I especially want to thank my eighth-grade English teacher, Mrs. Thurston, for instilling in me a deeper knowledge and understanding of the English language.

The biggest thank-you of all goes to all of the parents, peers, and students across the world who have encouraged me to write a book. And last, I want to thank the Uber drivers who spoke a tremendous deal of insight into my life and confirmed my dream to write this book with my dad.

ABOUT THE AUTHORS

Drew Formsma is widely known as a voice to his generation and a peer who can communicate with them unlike any adult. He began speaking with his dad in 2016 at the age of fourteen to audiences of tens of thousands of people around the world on the simple idea that generosity is the key to a better life. Drew lives in Southern California with his family and has set his sights on playing the top 100 golf courses in America by the age of forty.

Brad Formsma is the author of the award-winning book I Like Giving: The Transforming Power of a Generous Life and founder and president of ilikegiving.com, a movement which has inspired more than 100 million people in over 170 countries to live generously. Brad has been featured on *Today, Fox News, National Geographic* and *Forbes*. Brad speaks on leadership and organizational health for businesses including Trek Bicycle, Southeastern Freight Lines, Merrill Lynch and Johns Hopkins. Brad guides families through custom gatherings to help them discuss generosity together with every generation, so that their values and story live on. Brad and his wife Laura have three children and live in Southern California.

I LIKE GIVING

The Book

Named one of the top inspirational books of 2015, *I Like Giving* takes you through short stories of every kind of generosity and touches the heart of people ages 8 to 98. You will learn that giving is something you get to do—not something you've got to do—and there are small changes in your everyday life you can make that will create huge impact. One of the best gift books you'll find, you can order copies of *I Like Giving* at shopilikegiving.com.

Connect with Brad and Drew

Brad and Drew would love to hear from you!

Reach out to them at:

andrew1@ilikegiving.com

brad1@ilikegiving.com

Connect with @drewformsma on Twitter, Instagram, and Facebook

Connect with @bradformsma on Twitter and Instagram.

Follow @ilikegiving on Facebook, Twitter, and Instagram for daily inspiration.

EVERYDAY GENEROSITY

EVERYDAY GENEROSITY

_____

_____

_____

_____

_____

_____

_____

_____

_____

_____

_____

_____

_____

_____

_____

_____

_____

_____

_____

_____

EVERYDAY GENEROSITY

EVERYDAY GENEROSITY

_____

_____

_____

_____

_____

_____

_____

_____

_____

_____

_____

_____

_____

_____

_____

_____

_____

_____

_____

_____

_____

EVERYDAY GENEROSITY

_____

_____

_____

_____

_____

_____

_____

_____

_____

_____

_____

_____

_____

_____

_____

_____

_____

_____

_____

_____

_____

_____

_____

INTERESTED IN INVITING BRAD AND DREW TO YOUR CONFERENCE, CHURCH, OR FAMILY GATHERING?

Brad also engages with leading businesses to create a culture of generosity.
Their unique message inspires action and has created significant impact in groups across America.

CONNECT WITH BRAD AND DREW

BRAD1@ILIKEGIVING.COM
ANDREW1@ILIKEGIVING.COM

[Une certaine Madame de Vo*** a quitté l'amant de la Duchesse pour quelqu'un d'autre.]

Elle l'a donc pris! J'en suis fort aise, je vous jure, tant à cause de la liberté que cela vous rend, que parce qu'*un pareil choix achève de la définir*: car ne vous y trompez pas au moins, vous aviez eu de terribles précurseurs; et tels qu'en vérité il y avait, si vous me permettez de vous le dire, une sorte d'ignominie à leur succéder. (*Duch.*, p. 54; c'est nous qui soulignons)

Le ton badin que la Duchesse adopte à l'égard des liaisons des autres fait place au plus grand sérieux lorsqu'il s'agit d'elle-même et de l'estime qu'elle croit devoir lui revenir. De fait, et de même que chez les héroïnes cornéliennes de la maturité, il apparaît parfois que le souci de l'honneur fait place à la fascination exercée par le point d'honneur et à une certaine sclérose du concept de gloire.[6] La méfiance de la Duchesse vis-à-vis de l'abandon sexuel va jusqu'à l'extrême, car elle frappe de soupçon jusqu'aux rapports sexuels à l'intérieur du mariage même.

Après une liaison malheureuse avec Madame de Gr***, le mari de la Duchesse a "cru aimer" sa propre femme pendant deux années entières. Pourquoi celle-ci n'a-t-elle pas mis ce retour à profit et tenté de fixer l'époux volage? C'est qu'il prenait ce qui n'était que du goût pour de l'amour. Et par conséquent,

... sans compter des répugnances dont il pouvait ne m'être pas facile de triompher, il m'était beaucoup *moins important de garder son cœur que de me conserver son estime*. Tôt ou tard, de quelque prix que m'eût été le premier, il aurait toujours fallu qu'il me fût enlevé; il était nécessaire au bonheur de ma vie de me conduire avec lui de façon à ne pas altérer l'autre. (*Duch.*, p. 68; c'est nous qui soulignons)

La Marquise des *Lettres* avait cédé à la tentation de jouer le rôle d'amante avec son époux, pour prendre connaissance, au bout de deux ans, des infidélités de celui-ci; après une dernière tentative pour le reconquérir, elle s'était déterminée à renoncer à l'amour. La Duchesse se veut plus lucide. Et ce qui détermine sa conduite, c'est, bien plus qu'une incompatibilité physique qui constituerait un motif suffisant, un besoin absolu d'estime. Car l'amour physique est un révélateur impitoyable:

Tout ce qui, tant qu'un mari est amant, l'amuse et lui plaît dans sa femme, devient, pour lui autant de sujets de crainte, lorsqu'il cesse d'aimer; il est si rare qu'il ne nous punisse point, lorsqu'il a pu parvenir à nous l'inspirer, de cette même confiance qu'il a parfois si vivement sollicitée, que nous ne pouvons trop éviter d'en prendre. (*Duch.*, p. 68)[7]

Le refus de soi, fondé sur cette crainte de s'exposer au mépris-jalousie d'un mari qui n'aime plus, s'assortit de la tolérance avec laquelle la Duchesse envisage les multiples liaisons du Duc son époux. Bien plus, elle va jusqu'à émettre des suggestions à seule fin d'en prolonger la durée: ainsi, pour ramener à soi Monsieur de***, Madame de Gr***, sa maîtresse du moment, devrait feindre l'indifférence devant sa perte, recette d'autant plus efficace que, selon la Duchesse, son époux n'est pas véritablement amoureux de sa nouvelle conquête; de même, conseil dont profiteront Laclos et Madame de Merteuil, il n'est tel moyen de dé-goûter un partenaire devenu importun que de jouer vis-à-vis de lui la passion la plus outrée (*Duch.*, pp. 69 et 25).[8]

Obéissant aux mêmes motivations, la Duchesse se réserve un rôle de voyeur passablement actif dans les aventures amoureuses de son amant, en même temps qu'elle tente de faire sa fortune en le mariant, toute consciente qu'elle est—ou devrait être—du danger que présenterait un tel époux pour une jeune fille innocente. On voit alors que cette vertu, cette estime dont la Duchesse est si préoccupée, ne tendent pas moins qu'à perpétuer le système en vigueur, puisque, outre qu'il est amoureux ailleurs (c'est-à-dire d'elle), elle sait le Duc incapable de fidélité. Sa politique n'en reste pas moins invariable—à l'égard de l'époux comme de l'amant. Et d'ailleurs l'un est-il si différent de l'autre? N'est-il pas symptomatique que l'auteur les désigne l'un et l'autre par le même titre nobiliaire, quels que soient les risques de confusion qui peuvent en découler pour le lecteur?

L'époux et l'amant ne font qu'un, et c'est sur l'abandon aux pulsions du corps que porte la condamnation de l'héroïne: on refuse de voir l'autre aussi bien que d'être vue par lui, dans la mesure où l'on se révélerait pleinement à lui dans l'absence à soi qu'est la jouissance amoureuse, et la décision est prise et exécutée parce qu'on a soi-même trop vu. "Indifférence" et regard à distance—assorti de voyeurisme—sont d'ailleurs dans un rapport de causalité réciproque:

Forcée par mon indifférence à n'être que spectatrice, j'ai mis à observer un temps que je n'employais pas à sentir; et vous [son amant] devez trouver assez simple qu'il n'ait pas été absolument perdu pour mon instruction . . . . (*Duch.*, p. 96)

—"laquelle justifie à son tour mon désir de m'en tenir à mon indifférence initiale . . . ."

La règle vaut d'ailleurs pour la femme la plus raisonnable comme pour l'homme le plus libertin, puisque le motif de crainte ou de regret est, dans les deux cas, de s'être livré pleinement au regard de l'autre: le Clerval du *Hasard*, victime de Madame d'Olbray, le Versac des *Egarements*, le Chester des *Heureux Orphelins* ne sont pas moins conscients du ridicule, sanction de leur première aventure, que la femme faible ne l'est du mépris dont s'est assortie la sienne.[9]

Le Duc s'étant ouvertement déclaré, la Duchesse feint la surprise: sa vie amoureuse n'est-elle pas assez remplie, et n'est-il pas sur le point de remplacer Madame de Vo*** par Mademoiselle de Br***, témoignant une fois de plus des "droits" que la classe des "philosophes," à laquelle il appartient, a sur lui?

> ... et si je ne pouvais vous soupçonner d'ignorer à quel point celle-là mérite un si beau titre, ce n'en était pas plus pour moi une raison de croire qu'auprès d'elle le mépris vous sauvât du désir; et que même *ce n'en fût pas une de plus pour qu'elle vous en inspirât.* (*Duch.*, p. 105; c'est nous qui soulignons)

La preuve est là, en toutes lettres, de ce que nous avons avancé, à plusieurs reprises, à titre d'hypothèse: mépris et désir sont en rapport d'implication mutuelle et réciproque; si le désir satisfait engendre le mépris, il ne peut lui-même naître qu'à condition d'être engendré par lui. Le mépris est à la fois conséquence et condition préexistante du désir sexuel. Bien plus, ce mépris contaminera, au terme du roman, celle-là même dont l'unique souci avait été le maintien de sa "gloire": c'est précisément au moment où la Duchesse s'apprête à consentir à sa chute finale, en acceptant enfin de voir son amant, que les manœuvres par lesquelles la partenaire sexuelle de celui-ci tente de soumettre à publicité les deux liaisons—selon la tendresse, et selon le goût—du Duc, vont précipiter la rupture définitive.

Alors que dans l'économie crébillonienne canonique la satisfaction du désir éprouvé par un sujet A pour un sujet B entraîne, outre la publicité qui lui est accordée, la retombée du mépris de A sur son partenaire, au terme des *Lettres de la Duchesse* le mépris dont les diverses incarnations de B étaient de plus en plus justiciables vient à son tour frapper la femme estimable, et ce en dehors de tout commerce sexuel actualisé: le choix de certains objets de goût et la publicité qui en est inséparable constituent en eux-mêmes une irrécusable preuve de mépris à l'égard de l'objet de tendresse que, non content de se définir soi-même, on définit par contre-coup.

"L'on n'accorde jamais rien impunément à l'amour" (*Duch.*, p. 475)—ni au *goût* de l'autre pour les autres. Et si le mot "mépris" est absent de l'ultime lettre du recueil, le contexte dans lequel apparaît son antonyme ne saurait laisser planer de doute. Bien que la mort de son mari lui ait rendu sa liberté, la Duchesse refuse d'accéder à la demande en mariage du Duc— offre "à laquelle pourtant j'avoue que je suis sensible, parce qu'il ne se peut point que je ne le sois pas *à tout ce qui peut* me marquer de l'*estime* de votre part" (*Duch.*, p. 476; c'est nous qui soulignons). "Tout ce qui peut": entendons "si peu que ce soit." La discrétion de la litote antiphrastique s'efforce de masquer, pour ne l'en révéler que mieux, la conscience qu'a l'héroïne du mépris croissant[10] dont avait témoigné pour elle toute la conduite du Duc, et l'affirmation a valeur de *sentence* finale: "Recevoir de vos lettres, y répondre, était une manière de *vous trouver moins absent* que, de moi-même, je n'aurais pas cherchée; mais à laquelle, aussi, il était *naturel* que je ne me refusasse pas" (*Duch.*, p. 474; c'est nous qui soulignons). Non pas "compréhensible," ou "concevable," mais *naturel*. L'écriture amoureuse affirme à nouveau sa fonction de substitut érotique. Ecrire, c'est se rendre, et c'est s'exposer aux coups d'un mépris auquel la rapidité de sa circulation confère une quasi-ubiquité. Bien plus, et la Duchesse a failli en faire l'expérience à ses dépens, écrire, c'est s'exposer à circuler sous les espèces d'une correspondance investie par le désir: la publicité constitue ici encore le canal par lequel s'effectue la "métamorphose," ultime prix de l'oubli de soi-même pour tout sujet assez imprudent pour "accorder quelque chose à l'amour."

Il serait possible, dans une perspective psychologique, de débattre des motifs et du bien-fondé de la décision à laquelle s'astreint l'héroïne des *Lettres de la Duchesse*.[11] Est-ce sa lucidité, est-ce l'empire d'une crainte à présent insurmontable, qui la font se refuser à son amant, telle l'héroïne de Madame de Lafayette, telle surtout une incarnation en laquelle se fondraient les deux Bérénice tragiques?

"Votre cœur est à moi, j'y règne, c'est assez." Ainsi l'héroïne cornélienne prend-elle congé avant de s'exiler à jamais dans le silence d'un Orient discursif dont nous savons qu'il équivaut à la mort. La Duchesse se contente d'une assurance bien plus humble: "il ne se peut point que je ne sois pas sensible à tout ce qui peut me marquer de l'estime de votre part"—en d'autres termes: "il me suffit que vous ne me méprisiez pas tout à fait à l'instant même où vous me faites votre proposition." Car telle est la morale—déjà présente, mais adoucie, dans *Le Hasard*—des *Lettres de la Duchesse*: face à l'omnipotence du goût-mépris, c'est à présent l'*estime* qui est affaire de moment.

Si les *Lettres de la Duchesse* s'inscrivent rétrospectivement dans la tradition du conte merveilleux, il apparaît d'autre part qu'elles contiennent en germe des éléments auxquels *Les Liaisons dangereuses* de Choderlos de Laclos permettront de s'épanouir pleinement. Compte tenu de la différence de ton qui semble placer les deux romans aux antipodes l'un de l'autre, un tel jugement peut surprendre. Sans doute, en procédant à un recensement de détails ou notations minimes, est-il possible d'établir un lien de filiation entre deux œuvres quelles qu'elles soient, dans le cadre d'une intertextualité ponctuelle, fondée sur l'emprunt volontaire et conscient. Les ressemblances sont au contraire bien plus significatives lorsqu'elles portent sur des points qui touchent au système textuel, logique et/ou thématique sous-jacent aux ouvrages comparés. Il nous a donc paru nécessaire, avant d'entamer la section finale du présent chapitre, de ménager une pause consacrée à une brève comparaison des deux romans précités. Pause dont la présence au sein de cette étude devrait permettre au surplus de préciser encore l'étroite corrélation qui s'établit chez l'auteur du *Hasard* entre le jeu sur les concepts, d'une part, et le jeu sur les signifiants, de l'autre.

Il convient tout d'abord d'attirer l'attention sur la présence, dans les deux œuvres, du motif de la manipulation à distance. Sans doute la Duchesse est-elle fort éloignée du démonisme particulier à Madame de Merteuil. On a pourtant vu quelles conséquences néfastes son goût pour l'action à distance et par personne interposée a failli avoir sur des tiers innocents. Et dans les deux cas, le sort final de l'héroïne est le même, à savoir l'exil. On signalera de plus que la seconde partie des *Lettres* oppose à la Duchesse les machinations d'une figure féminine antagoniste, dont le caractère et les fonctions dans l'économie narrative préfigurent ceux dont Laclos investira Madame de Merteuil: Madame de LI*** est dangereuse, car elle joue—par désir de vengeance—avec la réputation des autres, et l'arme avec laquelle elle tente de détruire la Duchesse est précisément la menace de publication d'une partie de sa correspondance.

Madame de Merteuil ne serait-elle pas la synthèse des deux figures anta-gonistes des *Lettres*? A Madame de Li***—outre son indifférence vis-à-vis de la vertu—elle emprunte la méchanceté et le souci de détruire une rivale plus pure, tandis qu'elle retient de la Duchesse un goût de la manipulation et du voyeurisme,[12] dont l'exercice efficace repose essentiellement sur sa capacité à observer en silence les faibles et les ridicules d'un monde face auquel elle revendique à la fois sa supériorité et son autonomie.

Outre les ressemblances précitées au niveau des personnages, il convient d'accorder une attention particulière au fait que les deux romans partagent plusieurs motifs narratifs, dont celui du procès perdu par l'héroïne ou le héros libertin, mais surtout celui de la maladie de peau-châtiment, nous paraissent présenter un intérêt tout particulier, compte tenu des réseaux de signification dans lesquels ils viennent s'intégrer.

Telle est la réaction de la Duchesse à la nouvelle que Madame de Li*** vient de contracter la petite vérole:

... si c'était par un motif dont j'eusse à rougir, que je désirerais qu'elle devînt laide, je n'avouerais pas avec tant de franchise que je voudrais qu'il eût dit vrai, qu'elle eût la petite vérole, *qu'elle en revînt pourtant, mais le visage à faire trembler*. (*Duch.*, pp. 254-55; c'est nous qui soulignons)

On sait que la rétribution finale de l'héroïne des *Liaisons* a pu faire l'objet de condamnations diverses, fondées sur le goût de la demi-teinte et surtout d'une ambiguïté que certains souhaitaient plus prononcée chez un précur-seur du roman moderne. Nous ajouterons que cette même ambiguïté (dont l'absence en ce point ne nous gêne nullement dans les *Liaisons*) règne au contraire dans les *Lettres de la Duchesse*, où nous verrons qu'elle s'exerce, en l'espèce, selon des modalités particulièrement subtiles. Il nous paraît toutefois justifié de poser que l'obédience déjà mentionnée des *Lettres* à la grammaire fonctionnelle propre au genre merveilleux permet à son tour de replacer le roman de Laclos dans la lumière voulue et d'y voir également une version mondaine d'un conflit dont les enjeux—et peut-être les acteurs réels—relèvent d'une autre sphère. L'alliance instable des deux complices-antagonistes s'inscrit finalement dans une magie noire contre laquelle la magie blanche, bien affaiblie, de Madame de Rosemonde n'est pas de force. Et dans cette perspective la conclusion des *Liaisons* offre alors la contre-partie romanesque—et désabusée—de celle que ménageait dans le genre merveilleux *La Tyrannie des fées détruite* précitée.

Le visage ravagé de Madame de Merteuil, la perte de ce qui était à la fois masque et arme de séduction, répond comme en écho au crépuscule des "monstres" de *La Tyrannie*. En effet, ce qui doit disparaître avec elles n'est pas uniquement un pouvoir voué au mal, mais aussi un genre littéraire tout entier, lié au type de sensibilité qui avait permis sa floraison. Comme l'apparition, au terme de *La Tyrannie*, de la "divine princesse,"[13] allégorie littéraire de la jeune Duchesse de Bourgogne, met un terme aux enchantements d'un Versailles enfin rendu à l'empire de la jeunesse et de l'amour vertueux,[14] la victoire des valeurs incarnée dans *Les Liaisons* par la Présidente de Tourvel—ici encore "les armes cèdent à la magistrature"—sonne le glas des machinations du couple destructeur, mais surtout du récit libertin lui-même.

On voit alors de quelles multiples fonctions est investi le motif de la petite vérole: il intervient au niveau thématique de l'être et du paraître, du visage et du masque, et constitue le résidu "réaliste" de la métamorphose-châtiment propre au merveilleux. Il joue enfin un rôle essentiel, dans le cadre d'une thématique de l'éruption, émergence brutale d'un souterrain jusque-là réprimé. Chez Laclos, son occurrence vient doubler, en en soulignant la signification, la mort de Valmont et surtout la publication de lettres qui lui fait suite; par un transfert du social à l'individuel, du moral au physique, à la fièvre morale qui tenaillait sourdement le corps social succède, outre la révélation des trames sur lesquelles les deux conspirateurs avaient fondé leur pouvoir, l'éruption cutanée qui en constitue le terme symbolique.[15]

On connaît le prix d'une telle purge: Valmont et Tourvel morts, Merteuil en exil, ne subsiste alors qu'un vide terminal et aseptisé; ce "brave new world" est, d'une certaine façon, un monde épuisé où la mort prochaine de l'ancienne sagesse (Rosemonde, la "dernière fée") semble laisser le champ libre à la bêtise aveugle et bien pensante (Dancey, Volanges). La fin de "l'enchantement" révèle sa vraie nature, celle d'un désenchantement. Dans l'ère nouvelle dont la conclusion du roman est en même temps l'aube sur le plan du récit comme sur celui de l'*Histoire*, la "tyrannie" des fées comme celle des femmes a bien été détruite;[16] le pouvoir passe désormais à l'homme bourgeois et raisonnable.

Si Laclos opère par élimination, Crébillon opère par exclusion: le monde et son train intouchés, c'est l'héroïne elle-même qui s'exile. D'autre part, la thématique de l'éruption liée au défigurement n'apparaît, dans les *Lettres de la Duchesse*, que sur un mode atténué; le vœu de l'héroïne comme les machinations de Madame de Li*** resteront sans effets sensibles: l'une conservera sa beauté, l'autre sa réputation (ni son nom ni ses lettres ne seront publiés). Est-ce à dire que les éléments ci-dessus mentionnés ne figureraient dans le roman que pour y remplir une fonction thématique coupée de toute fonction de nature causale? Eu égard aux résultats précédemment fournis par notre examen du *Hasard*, un tel état de choses apparaîtrait comme profondément anormal, puisqu'il contredirait la règle selon laquelle, compte tenu de l'étroite interdépendance entre le narratif et le causal, nulle coupure ne saurait s'instaurer entre unités thématiques et unités narratives.

Sans doute, l'héroïne échappe à l'exposition de son discours amoureux, mais c'est pour disparaître à jamais avec lui du champ du monde et du désir: tel est le prix qu'elle doit payer pour écarter les risques d'éruption dont nous parlions plus haut. Ce que l'on doit cependant souligner, c'est que cet exil correspond à une sorte de mise en quarantaine à la fois volontaire et forcée: par le biais d'une conversion similaire à celle dont il a été fait état pour *Les Liaisons dangereuses*, mais se réalisant en sens inverse, la maladie physique dont Madame de Li*** a réchappé, mais sur laquelle le mépris de la Duchesse fondait tant d'espérances, vient à présent, et par l'intermédiaire du Duc lui-même,[17] contaminer l'héroïne dans le champ éthique et moral. On pourrait même parler de retour du mépris-maladie,[18] dans la mesure où, par une double transposition du moral au physique, puis du physique au moral, le mépris qui frappe la Duchesse au terme du roman est celui-là même qu'elle avait exprimé dans la lettre sur la petite vérole de Madame de Li***. Si donc l'éruption deux fois espérée—par l'héroïne et par sa rivale —n'a pas lieu, la "maladie" subsiste à l'état endémique, dans le corps mondain comme dans l'âme individuelle. En l'absence de symptômes manifestes, la seule conséquence de cet épisode de la chronique mondaine sera tout au plus un accès bénin de "fièvre froide". . . . Quant à la Duchesse, si dans sa dernière lettre elle laisse tomber le masque en révélant au Duc l'étendue de son amour passé, c'est pour dérober à jamais son "cœur" et son "esprit" sous le voile d'un silence éternel.

Il se confirme une fois de plus que le monde selon Crébillon a la nature d'un circuit où circule la valeur mépris/estime, selon des modalités et des directions qui sont fonctions de la perspective morale dont l'auteur fait élection: à l'optimisme relatif de la perspective "libertine" s'oppose le pessimisme de la perspective "tendre." On vient de voir par ailleurs qu'à côté d'une transmission s'effectuant dans le cadre d'une isotopie économique proprement dite et selon les modalités de l'avoir, du prendre, du donner et du garder, en apparaît une seconde, située cette fois dans l'isotopie de la maladie et de la contagion. Le mépris s'acquerrait comme une affection corporelle pure et simple: "ils n'en mouraient pas tous, mais tous étaient frappés." Il est d'ailleurs possible—et sans doute souhaitable—de procéder à un regroupement des deux isotopies sous l'unique égide d'un "don" qu'on prendrait dans la signification qui lui revient traditionnellement dans le champ ethnologique, d'un *gift* dont la langue anglaise et la langue allemande révèlent les deux significations opposées et cependant complémentaires; support d'un transfert dont on connaît l'absence ultime de gratuité, il est en même temps poison qui tue si l'on ne s'en décharge pas sur quelqu'un d'autre: tout don est empoisonné.

Mais l'intensité et les effets du poison varient selon le sujet considéré et son attitude à l'égard du monde qui l'enserre: car si celui-ci conserve en son sein les femmes légères dont il accélère la circulation après les avoir successivement—et légèrement—contaminées, il expulse définitivement, après une contamination brutale, la prude et la tendre dont il châtie ainsi non seulement les tergiversations vis-à-vis de leurs propres désirs, mais surtout les velléités d'autonomie dont elles se sont rendues coupables à son propre égard: la Marquise du *Hasard* conservera le Duc pour avoir doublement joué le jeu du monde, la Duchesse des *Lettres* le perdra à jamais pour s'y être trop longtemps refusée.

Est-ce à dire qu'une telle interprétation procède d'une approche métaphorique qui, propre au seul critique, lui fournirait une figure dont le pittoresque rendrait plus aisément compte du matériau textuel soumis à description? Nous considérons, bien au contraire, que l'œuvre de Crébillon elle-même révèle une omniprésence du thème de la contagion en tant que modalité de transmission métaphorique, et qu'il est donc possible de la soumettre à examen dans le cadre d'une isotopie proprement *clinique*.

A l'appui de cette assertion nous proposerons, pour conclure ce dernier chapitre, l'examen d'un épisode généralement négligé—parce que trop rapidement lu—du *Sopha*. On verra par ailleurs que cet épisode, outre qu'il réserve une fonction essentielle à la maladie physique, fournit l'un des témoignages les plus spectaculaires de la duplicité propre à l'auteur au niveau de la manipulation du sens, en même temps qu'il contribue à resserrer encore les éléments constitutifs du système érotico-économique tout entier.

L'épisode de la courtisane Amine est intercalé entre le premier, l'histoire de Fatmé, consacrée à l'activité sexuelle en ce qu'elle a de plus primaire et de plus brutal, et l'histoire de Phénime, où la tendresse s'exprime sous sa forme la plus utopique. Dans l'un la sexualité de l'héroïne est la plus proche qui soit de la nature, fondée qu'elle est sur un besoin exclusivement physique et sur l'utilisation égoïste de l'autre en tant qu'instrument propre à procurer la satisfaction recherchée; dans l'autre les pulsions empruntent le véhicule d'un amour-tendresse dont l'avènement est rendu possible par le double sacrifice préalablement consenti par chacun des deux amants.

L'histoire d'Amine explore un champ différent, celui de l'amour vénal où les prestations sexuelles ont pour contrepartie des contre-prestations de nature monétaire, elles-mêmes évaluées à la lumière du concept de valeur. C'est dire qu'alors que les deux autres épisodes se déroulent en marge du monde et de ses lois, celui-ci se place explicitement à l'intérieur du contexte fourni par un système économique authentique, celui d'un marché de biens et services. Sans doute celui-ci se situe-t-il théoriquement en marge du monde pris dans son acception la plus stricte. Est-ce à dire que l'univers des courtisanes et la sphère mondaine soient incommensurables l'une à l'autre? On va voir qu'il n'en est rien.

On sait déjà dans quelle mesure l'amour vénal proprement dit et le "goût" mondain sont susceptibles d'assimilation, dans la mesure où ils excluent tous deux la gratuité. La femme "galante" se fait rétribuer de son abandon en un temps de parole dont l'actualisation dépend de l'espoir de gain (plaisir physique, vanité, réputation) nourri par chacune des parties; la courtisane fournit ses services contre une somme d'argent dont le montant est fonction de la dépense à laquelle son client est disposé à consentir. Dans les deux cas, la valeur de la contre-prestation est définie à partir d'une Bourse dont l'aire d'activité et les membres constituants peuvent différer, mais dont les principes de fonctionnement restent les mêmes.

Résumons l'intrigue: tirée de sa condition médiocre par son nouveau protecteur, le grossier Abdalathif, Amine réintègre sa misère initiale après la découverte de ses multiples infidélités par son amant. Au terme d'une période de réflexion et de repentir présumés, un nouvel amateur, étranger à la ville et ignorant du "mépris" dans lequel elle y est tenue, la relance enfin dans le circuit de l'amour vénal.

Une telle histoire justifie-t-elle qu'on y consacre une étude détaillée, compte tenu de sa banalité et de l'absence de tout élément nouveau susceptible d'enrichir l'analyse du système crébillonien? Il est certain que le lecteur pressé n'en retirera qu'un ennui qui confirmerait, dans le cadre de l'épisode particulier, le bien-fondé de tel jugement porté sur *Le Sopha* pris dans sa totalité:

> La machine de ce long "roman" est si réduite et si pesante à la fois, les anecdotes si plates, les rebondissements du dialogue si nuls qu'on n'arrive à la fin de la lecture que parce qu'il faut bien qu'un livre soit ouvert ou fermé.[19]

Il apparaît toutefois que la banalité de l'épisode considéré relève—pour des raisons dont nous rendrons compte en leur temps—du leurre, et qu'il est impossible de n'y voir qu'une fade démarcation, orientalisée pour les besoins de la cause, d'une tradition exploitée avec plus de vigueur par un Lesage. L'histoire d'Amine est en fait l'un des exemples les plus frappants de la subtilité et de l'agilité propres à l'art crébillonien, en même temps que de l'ambiguïté-duplicité qui en constitue, à des niveaux divers, l'un des traits essentiels.

Sans doute le récit reprend-il fidèlement les termes propres du couple antithétique priser-estimer/mépriser. Ce qu'on doit voir, c'est que cette reprise est simultanément assortie d'un glissement de signification, en conformité logique avec le milieu socio-économique dépeint, mais—et c'est là le point le plus intéressant—partiel: si le prix des faveurs de la courtisane est d'ordre pécuniaire, le mépris auquel l'exposent ses infidélités et sa rapacité relève, lui, de la sphère morale. Il y a là un jeu—un "bâillement," si l'on veut—dans la signification, lequel devra à son tour aiguiser l'attention d'un lecteur déjà sensible au principe selon lequel, chez Crébillon, tout détail, aussi infime soit-il, est susceptible de s'intégrer dans un système discursif global dont il constitue souvent le principe moteur fondamental. C'est alors —et alors seulement—qu'il s'avère que cette première duplicité du signifiant en engendre à son tour une seconde, laquelle, soigneusement camouflée par un auteur qui fait peut-être trop confiance à son lecteur, confère à l'épisode tout le sel qu'un parcours hâtif inciterait à lui dénier.

Comme Socrate et le discours rabelaisien auquel celui-ci sert d'emblème, ce texte crébillonien particulier est un Silène qu'il faut savoir ouvrir, mais —ainsi qu'on va le voir—un Silène à l'envers.

A l'ouverture de l'épisode, l'âme punie d'Amanzéi (à la fois spectateur et narrateur des histoires-récits dont se compose *Le Sopha*), s'installe dans le sopha de la jeune courtisane: "sopha qui, terni, délabré, témoignait assez que c'était à ses dépens qu'on avait acquis les autres meubles qui l'accompagnaient" (*Sopha*, p. 46). Le sopha joue, à plus d'un titre, le rôle d'indice: en même temps que sa présence annonce, de par les connotations dont elle est porteuse, le point de départ d'un nouveau récit libertin, un lien logique s'établit entre le délabrement du meuble et les activités érotiques qui en sont la cause ainsi que les objets dont le produit de celles-ci a permis de faire l'acquisition. Contiguïté et substitution combinent leurs effets pour superposer à la métaphore prise dans son sens étymologique, et constituée par l'errance, de sopha en sopha, de l'âme spectatrice, une authentique métamorphose assortie d'un phénomène de multiplication des objets: de même que chaque déplacement d'Amanzéi donne prétexte à un récit—à un sopha—nouveau, chaque utilisation de son sopha par Amine entraîne, en contrepartie d'une perte de substance de celui-ci, une transformation de cette substance en objets supplémentaires qui viennent à leur tour se placer dans son voisinage. Toute acquisition se retrouve à son alentour sous des espèces différentes, mais dont la valeur globale répond à celle dont l'usure a privé le meuble central.

D'autre part, on peut dire que tous les meubles de la chambre racontent une histoire, soit "en plein" par leur seule présence—l'ameublement "périphérique"—soit "en creux"—le délabrement-manque du sopha, meuble "central." Bien plus, outre que cette même histoire apparaît sous deux manifestations différentes, ces dernières sont elles-mêmes concentriques l'une à l'autre, l'histoire "en creux" étant enchâssée dans l'autre, dont elle est à la fois l'équivalent et le principe générateur. Ce que l'on a ici, c'est en fait une mise en abyme d'une grande subtilité de l'un des principes constitutifs du *Sopha* considéré dans son intégralité: celui d'un enchâssement-*embedding*[20] non seulement statique mais encore génératif. Cette mise en abyme consiste en une description d'un espace physique, d'un système d'objets intradiégétique équivalant à la structure diégétique de l'œuvre tout entière, que des emboîtements multiples finissent par rattacher à une dimension spatiale qui vient se superposer à la dimension temporelle propre au discours narratif. En effet, le sopha-prison en même temps que l'ameublement qui l'environne, est, autant que meuble-indice, meuble-récit, témoin de récits passés et principe générateur du récit qui va se dérouler. Celui-ci, narré par Amanzéi, va s'insérer à son tour dans l'ensemble de niveau supérieur que constitue *Le Sopha*, fragment d'un *corpus* pseudo-historique consacré au règne fictif de Schah-Baham et, fondamentalement, au récit d'une narration destinée à distraire un potentat stupide.

L'activité sexuelle trouve ici sa compensation dans des contre-prestations monétaires. Celles-ci se métamorphosent elles-mêmes en un décor qui s'affirme comme valant-pour à la fois métonymique et métaphorique des épisodes érotiques en ayant permis la constitution. En remontant de l'effet à la cause fondamentale, on peut alors se demander si, dans la double optique de la métaphore-métamorphose, les sophas de Crébillon ne constituent pas, à un niveau plus profond que celui d'un simple "truc" de narration, les précurseurs des bijoux de Diderot, qui désignent, on le sait, par métaphore, l'organe sexuel féminin, et par métonymie, l'usage qu'elles en font. Bijou ou sopha d'Amine, c'est, dans les deux cas, d'un creux, d'un manque, que jaillit la parole—et le récit.[21] La subtilité est d'ailleurs plus prononcée chez Crébillon, puisque le processus métaphorique, non content de se réaliser par l'intermédiaire d'un simple mot, par une substitution de lexèmes, recourt de plus à une substitution d'objets: le sopha symbolise l'activité sexuelle de la courtisane non pas par l'affectation arbitraire d'un terme donné à une réalité qu'il ne recouvre pas normalement, mais par un double glissement: ce glissement conduit à identifier une partie du corps féminin à l'objet qui lui est contigu dans l'espace et qui, d'autre part, fournit le terrain approprié à ses ébats.

L'activité propre à l'héroïne de l'épisode considéré contribue bien évidemment à attirer l'attention du lecteur sur le lien indissoluble entre sexualité, économie et narration. La vénalité de la courtisane est d'ailleurs doublée par celle de son protecteur, dans lequel elle trouve un homologue masculin digne d'elle. Ce Turcaret oriental, non content d'exploiter le monde qui consent à frayer avec lui, l'a véritablement mis en carte dans la mesure où la tolérance dont il y bénéficie est la conséquence d'un achat de faveurs: "Tel qu'il était cependant, on le ménageait, non qu'il pût nuire, mais il savait obliger" (*Sopha*, p. 48). Bel euphémisme: le terme réfère pudiquement à des transactions essentiellement onéreuses. Le verbe "obliger" se prête d'ailleurs, au plus haut point, à ce double jeu, puisqu'il peut renvoyer tant à une dispensation de faveurs fondée sur la générosité du donateur qu'aux effets escomptés du don octroyé, c'est-à-dire à l'obligation incombant au bénéficiaire de fournir une contre-prestation de valeur égale, à manifester sa gratitude par une conduite concrète: en l'occurrence, cette gratitude est soumise à tarification, et, d'un côté comme de l'autre, le don gracieux n'est en fait que le déguisement d'une contribution à l'exécution d'un contrat à titre onéreux. Dans l'Agra du *Sopha*, tout est à vendre, la position sociale comme les faveurs sexuelles des femmes, quelles qu'elles soient, et, dans cet épisode tout au moins, la prostitution est partout la règle.

En témoigne la leçon d'économie dispensée par Abdalathif à sa protégée:

Rien ne perd tant les personnes de votre condition que ces étourderies que j'ai entendu nommer complaisances gratuites. Quand on sait qu'une fille est dans la malheureuse habitude de se donner pour rien, tout le monde croit être fait pour l'avoir à bon marché. (*Sopha*, p. 51)

Mais il ne s'agit pas seulement des "personnes de la condition d'Amine." Le narrateur ne pose une antithèse entre les femmes qui composent le monde et celles qui en sont exclues que pour mieux la nier; dans la société d'Agra les deux se valent, et dans l'œuvre de Crébillon la courtisane n'est autre que l'un des avatars métaphoriques possibles de la femme dite de qualité—l'autre étant, nous l'avons vu, la fée. On peut ainsi lire le récit dont Amine est la douteuse héroïne comme une sorte de transposition ou encore de réinstrumentation de la mélodie fondamentale que l'auteur du *Sopha* n'a cessé de varier tout au long de sa carrière. Mais ce qui renforce l'artifice de la transposition, c'est que la nature partielle de celle-ci permet d'accentuer, par le biais d'une parodie volontairement en porte à faux, les traits distinctifs propres au modèle parodié. L'efficacité d'un procédé qui repose sur la disparité, déjà mentionnée, des isotopies propres aux deux termes du couple priser/mépriser est manifeste dans la citation qui va suivre. Ayant trop bien profité de la leçon d'économie de son protecteur, Amine s'apprête incontinent à le tromper avec un jeune roué, dont elle tente de tirer le plus d'argent possible, tout en prétendant lui céder par inclination. On lui fait grâce de la comédie. Bien plus:

...je te paie même aussi cher que si j'étais en premier, et tu sais bien que ce n'est pas dans les règles.
—Il me semble que si, répondit Amine, je fais une perfidie pour vous et ...
—Si je ne te payais, interrompit-il, qu'à raison de ce qu'elle te coûte, je te réponds que je t'aurais pour rien. (*Sopha*, p. 65)

L'échange ci-dessus reprend au sens propre une terminologie dont on a déjà examiné l'emploi figuré dans le cadre de l'amour mondain, mais laisse coexister, par une incongruïté révélatrice, les deux isotopies morale ("inclination," "perfidie") et monétaire ("payer," "coûter," "avoir pour rien"). A l'ironie ménagée par le texte correpond d'ailleurs celle dont Abdalathif accable ses conquêtes dans les deux sphères où il évolue de concert. Le financier joue en effet sur les deux tableaux: il achète et vend ses faveurs dans les deux sphères, apparemment antithétiques, qu'il hante. Sensible aux plaisirs de l'alternance, il déserte parfois les boudoirs pour trouver ailleurs "des plaisirs qui, pour en être moins brillants, n'en étaient pas moins vifs et (selon ce qu'il avait l'insolence d'en dire) souvent guère plus dangereux" (*Sopha*, p. 48). Les deux dernières constructions comparatives négatives constituent, en une volute stylistique typique de l'auteur, une double affirmation d'équivalence: qu'on fréquente les femmes du monde ou les autres, les plaisirs comme les risques sont les mêmes.

Compte tenu de l'isotopie de la vénalité qui s'affirme dans la première section de l'épisode, il peut sembler que ce risque soit d'ordre économique et, dans les deux cas, exclusivement pécuniaire: si la grossièreté d'Abdalathif exclut qu'il puisse obtenir les faveurs des femmes de qualité par l'investissement que constitueraient des discours tournés selon les règles, on sait qu'en revanche il sait "obliger."

Compte tenu, d'autre part, de la fidélité de la courtisane aux théories économiques—sinon à la personne—de son protecteur, et de l'application qu'elle leur donnera par le biais de multiples aventures strictement tarifées en fonction de la race, de la religion de ses partenaires, ou encore de ses remords présumés, il semble que l'épisode doive fonctionner jusqu'à son terme selon les règles du jeu précédemment dégagées.

C'est alors qu'Abdalathif apprend la vérité sur la conduite d'Amine, mais dans des conditions que le narrateur se refuse à exploiter. Tout au plus, par le biais d'éliminations successives, Amanzéi écartera les hypothèses de la dénonciation et de la découverte par surprise, émises par Schah-Baham (son narrataire): "Point du tout, Sire, répartit Amanzéi; il aurait été trop heureux d'en être quitte à si bon compte" (*Sopha*, p. 67). L'inception et le dénouement d'une liaison de ce type passent donc par la même procédure: dans les deux cas, il faut payer le juste prix—et le narrateur indique expressément que le financier paie cher. Quel est donc l'événement "imprévu quoiqu'il n'fût pas sans exemple" (ibid.) qui le tire de son aveuglement? Il faut ici rapprocher ces deux périphrases de la double périphrase, précitée, par laquelle Abdalathif exprimait son opinion sur les avantages et inconvénients respectifs de ses deux carrières libertines parallèles. Le rapprochement permet alors de concevoir que l' "événement" en question ne saurait être que la réalisation du "danger" auquel il était fait allusion plus haut—et l' "insolence" d'Abdalathif se révèle dans toute son étendue. On doit en effet admettre que ce danger qui n'est pas moindre chez les femmes de qualité que chez les prostituées, n'est autre que celui de contracter une maladie vénérienne!

La révélation est en même temps punition, Abdalathif apprenant à ses dépens que les courtisanes sont *tout de même* plus dangereuses que leurs concurrentes . . . .

On doit noter que la surprise de la victime risque fort de ne pas être doublée d'un effet de surprise du côté du lecteur. Car si la stratégie narrative superpose aux isotopies selon lesquelles elle se développait jusque-là une isotopie supplémentaire que l'on définira comme clinique, ce n'est qu'avec une discrétion malicieuse qu'elle procède à la mise en place de ce jeu second entre moral-économique et physique, entre les vices de l'esprit —et des contrats—et les affections du corps. Et ce n'est qu'une fois en possession de la clef en question que le lecteur pourra décrypter la dernière section de l'épisode, dont l'écriture lui révélera le codage auquel elle a été systématiquement soumise. Son travail de décodage tendra alors à la restitution d'une isotopie clinique qu'occulte patiemment—sauf en un point précis, lequel constituera une confirmation indiscutable de notre hypothèse de lecture—le recours à une terminologie afférente à la sphère éthique et morale.

On trouvera un premier exemple de la nécessité et des résultats d'une double lecture, à la fois re-lecture et lecture à deux niveaux—dans la menace qu'Abdalathif adresse à la coupable: "on saura vous apprendre à être sage, et vous mettre en un lieu où vous serez forcée de l'être, du moins quelque temps" (*Sopha*, p. 69). Compte tenu de l'isotopie sous-morale déjà établie, le lecteur naïf pensera, bien évidemment, à un établissement du type de la Salpêtrière (rendu célèbre par le récit de Prévost), prison pour filles galantes. Mais le lecteur conscient de la duplicité du texte—et il était sans doute plus facile de l'être à un contemporain de Crébillon qu'au lecteur du XXe siècle—se remémorera qu'un tel "lieu" est, avant d'être une prison, un hôpital: les motifs de salubrité publique qui dictent la mise à l'écart d'une Amine temporairement "assagie," relèvent ici d'un souci d'hygiène bien plus physique que moral; il s'agit tout simplement de mettre hors circuit un agent de contamination certaine, et non pas de punir une infidélité au code des conduites contractuelles.

Cette même lecture révélera d'autre part tout le sel de la grande scène où, Abdalathif ayant excipé de l'existence de "témoins"[22] convaincants à l'appui de ses accusations, Amine, selon une tactique caractéristique de l'héroïne crébillonienne, décide d'abandonner le terrain de la justification pour celui de la contre-attaque: sans doute Abdalathif a-t-il "raison de se plaindre," mais si elle croit "devoir à son tour l'accabler de reproches sur ses infidélités, lui faire même des remonstrances sur le mauvais choix qu'il faisait" (*Sopha*, p. 70), ce n'est nullement pour jouer le jeu classique—et inadéquat en l'espèce—de la femme moralement outragée, mais bien pour rejeter sur d'autres la responsabilité de la contagion qu'on fait peser sur elle.

Le narrateur n'en persistant pas moins à maintenir le voile qu'il a préalablement jeté sur la réalité des choses, la conclusion de l'épisode offre une magistrale démonstration de l'habileté narrative et verbale de l'auteur; en même temps le jeu auquel celui-ci soumet les diverses isotopies sus-mentionnées va se résoudre en ce qui, selon nous, relève encore une fois d'une activité authentiquement métaphorique, tendant à intégrer dans une relation réversible comparant-comparé, le champ de la maladie du corps et celui des vices de l'esprit:

Je ne vous dirai pas ce qu'il avait, mais jamais je n'ai vu d'homme plus fâché. Ce dont il était le plus outré, c'est qu'on eût osé *manquer* d'une façon si cruelle à ce qu'on *devait* à un homme comme lui. (*Sopha*, p. 71; c'est nous qui soulignons)

Cette déclaration du narrateur superpose une fois de plus deux isotopies dépourvues de point de contact commun: manquer et devoir appartiennent certes aux deux sphères morale et économique, mais nous savons que la fidélité dont Amine était redevable à son protecteur n'était qu'une contre-prestation contribuant à l'exécution d'un contrat à objet purement sexuel

et par ailleurs rémunéré. La surface du texte propose la manifestation ironi-
que d'un sens qu'elle dissimule de façon absolument concertée—"je ne vous
dirai pas ce qu'il avait . . ."—et le discours narratif va jongler à présent avec
trois isotopies à la fois, dont chacune des deux premières—contractuelle et
éthico-morale—aura pour fonction de camoufler la troisième. Les mots
feront alors office d'écran, et leur opacité, leur pouvoir de gazage varieront
en fonction de l'acuité de regard du lecteur. Car tel est l'un des principes
de l'art libertin: présenter au regard une surface unie, auquel il appartiendra
au consommateur perspicace de restituer le relief originel. Il incombera
donc à celui-ci de décrypter des termes tels que "mortification," "humilia-
tion," "honte" (*Sopha*, p. 72), de même que de démêler—et d'apprécier à
sa juste valeur—l'ambiguïté de la périphrase "la réputation d'une personne
peu sûre dans le commerce" (*Sopha*, p. 73). On voit que l'auteur s'y joue
avec virtuosité de la double signification d'un terme qui se réfère à la fois
à une activité de communication gratuite dans la sphère amoureuse ou
mondaine, et à une activité marchande fondée sur l'échange et la circulation de biens et valeurs dans la sphère non mondaine.[23] Le jeu est significa-
tif: par delà l'héroïne elle-même, il a valeur de constat sur la transformation
en "boutique" du "monde" qui peuple Agra. Si donc le texte paraît perver-
tir le sens comme à plaisir, c'est précisément parce que ce sens a d'ores
et déjà été soumis à distorsion dans l'ordre référentiel fictif qu'est censé
dépeindre *Le Sopha*, voire dans l'ordre référentiel dont ce dernier est censé
être le reflet littéraire. Perversion du sens au sein du monde, perversion du
sens aussi dans les rapports entre membres des deux sexes: on sait à présent
en quoi consiste la "tendresse" que le robuste Mahmoud persiste à témoi-
gner à sa maîtresse au cours de la période de chômage forcé qu'elle doit
traverser.[24]

Ainsi que nous l'avons annoncé plus haut, c'est en un point unique de
cette toute dernière partie de l'épisode que le narrateur livre explicitement
la clef de l'énigme, mais si furtivement que le lecteur pressé ou innocent—
chez Crébillon le premier et le second sont d'ailleurs en rapport d'implication—sera dans l'impossibilité d'en tirer un quelconque parti. La retraite à
laquelle la "mauvaise opinion" qu'on avait d'elle a forcé la courtisane prend
fin; avec le temps "on la crut changée, on imagina que les réflexions qu'on
lui avait laissé le temps de faire l'avait *guérie* de la fureur d'être infidèle.
Les amants revinrent" (*Sopha*, p. 74; c'est nous qui soulignons). Mais telle
est la duplicité d'un discours systématiquement fondé sur une *klassische
Dämpfung* poussée à la limite que, par un tour de passe-passe sémantique,
et eu égard à la pression exercée par l'isotopie morale de surface, le mot
révélateur "guérie" ne suggérera son sens propre au lecteur que pour le
recouvrir aussitôt de son sens figuré ("corrigée," "repentante").

Il est donc aisé de mettre sur le compte des "réflexions" ce qui relève de l'action curative présumée du mercure.[25] Bien plus, non content de jouer avec les significations, le texte, par son recours aux verbes "croire" et "imaginer," laisse à dessein planer le doute sur la réalité du rétablissement de la jeune courtisane. Amine est-elle effectivement guérie? Sans doute rentre-t-elle dans le circuit érotique grâce à un nouveau protecteur qui, étranger à la ville, ignore tout de ses antécédents: "[il] acheta au plus haut prix des faveurs qui dans Agra commençaient à être taxées *au plus bas*, et n'étaient pourtant pas encore aussi *méprisées* qu'elles auraient dû l'être" (*Sopha*, p. 74; c'est nous qui soulignons). Tel est le contexte dans lequel apparaît le terme autour duquel le présent chapitre s'est constitué. Mais s'insérant dans la polysémie concertée de ce contexte particulier, c'est pour en participer aussitôt. Car le mépris, c'est le jugement moral qu'on passe sur l'individu indigne d'estime; c'est aussi dans l'isotopie marchande les diminutions de prix auxquelles doivent consentir ceux ou celles qui sont "peu sûrs" dans le commerce.[26] C'est enfin et surtout l'équivalent métaphorique, dans l'isotopie morale, de la maladie dans l'isotopie clinique. Et dans cette dernière isotopie, le texte laisse entendre qu'Amine n'est *toujours pas* guérie: le mépris dont on devrait sanctionner ses faveurs, n'est autre que l'état de quarantaine sexuelle dans lequel on devrait la maintenir.

Au contraire, la jeune courtisane échappe à l'immobilisation-dépréciation qui devrait être son lot pour réintégrer le grand circuit érotique—avec la maladie dont elle est porteuse. Maladie qui va, par la même occasion, intensifier d'autant plus l'arbitraire des tarifications dont elle avait coutume d'assortir ses services, et ce jusqu'à modifier irréductiblement l'*objet* du contrat lui-même: car ce qu'on achète à présent d'Amine, c'est une maladie vénérienne.

"Hélas," s'était écriée en un jeu de mots révélateur la mère de la jeune courtisane: "nous sommes bien punies de nous être fiées à un infidèle" (*Sopha*, p. 70). C'est peut-être en effet d'un infidèle—c'est-à-dire un étranger à la communauté de croyance propre à la ville—qu'Amine, elle-même infidèle à son protecteur tout en étant trop fidèle à ses préceptes, tient la maladie dont elle est porteuse. Et compte tenu du supplément qu'elle lui a fait payer, cette maladie est, dans tous les sens, le prix de l'infidélité. Arbitraire du prix et maladie sont ainsi dans un rapport nécessaire. A contracter vicieusement, on ne peut que contracter une maladie honteuse.

Le délabrement initial du sopha n'était pas qu'indice d'une profession présente, ou équivalent métaphorique de la vertu de son utilisatrice; il était déjà symptôme prophétique du délabrement final du corps de l'héroïne, de son protecteur ainsi que des successeurs qu'elle va lui donner. Comme le sopha d'Amine, le corps d'Abdalathif a "témoigné" (cf. les "témoins" de la

p. 70) que c'est "à ses dépens" qu'Amine a arrondi son petit pécule. Et le manque d'où naît le récit constitue en même temps une préfiguration de ce que sera sa conclusion: un manque supplémentaire, infligé par la contagion à ce qui reste d'intégrité au corps individuel et social. Le discours narratif simule par surcroît au niveau de l'expression ce qu'il pose et développe au niveau du contenu; les jeux sur les signifiants et leurs isotopies, c'est-à-dire les creux, les espaces que les lexèmes laissent s'entrebâiller entre leurs signifiés possibles, viennent à leur tour se superposer—en les reflétant —aux jeux de la communication qui s'instaurent dans la dimension syntagmatique. Le texte tout entier se révèle alors comme l'image-miroir englobante des corps qui le peuplent: il est, lui aussi, le lieu d'une dialectique du dedans et du dehors, du latent et du manifeste. Lui aussi investi par un signifié-maladie secret et honteux, il en propose tout à la fois le dépistage à la perspicacité du lecteur, par ces quelques mots-symptômes, "témoins" si discrets qu'il est possible d'en ignorer la présence, mais une fois celle-ci reconnue, indubitablement "convaincants."[27]

Dans l'économie propre à l'épisode considéré, le sopha-meuble se manifeste encore plus clairement comme le siège d'une perte qu'occulterait un gain apparent—celui du plaisir sexuel ou de l'argent qui le rétribue—ou mieux encore un gain négatif. Et si l'art rhétorique propre au *Sopha*-récit dissimule ici la maladie du corps par le recours à un vocabulaire tout entier —sauf en ce point révélateur où le corps et son affection parlent—affecté à la sphère morale, il s'avère au surplus que la métaphore à laquelle aboutit le jeu soutenu sur les mots et leurs signifiés est à son tour parfaitement réversible. En effet, si les affections vénériennes contractées par les courtisanes et les symptômes physiques qu'elles causent chez les clients de celles-ci justifient le "mépris," la dévaluation qui doit frapper leurs services, à l'inverse et dans la sphère des valeurs éthiques et mondaines, le mépris et le ridicule ont valeur et fonction de symptômes moraux d'une "maladie sociale" dont l'étude des *Lettres de la Duchesse* a explicité le fonctionnement.

Au niveau rhétorique, on est donc en présence d'un tourniquet métaphorique dans lequel comparant et comparé sont susceptibles d'échanger indéfiniment leurs positions. Comme il le faisait déjà dans le cadre de l'antithèse, Crébillon n'investit de signifiés particuliers les termes d'une relation logique que pour mieux nier en tout ou en partie la validité du principe fondamental d'altérité—A n'est pas B—sur lequel des figures comme la métaphore ou l'antithèse dépendent pour leur fonctionnement. Le chaud et le froid sont théoriquement termes contradictoires, mais en tant qu'ils sont utilisés figurativement, ils entrent dans une double relation d'identité (le chaud transit, le froid brûle) et d'implication (le froid du mépris implique le chaud du goût, lequel à son tour implique la préexistence du froid du mépris). De même, dans le cadre de la relation métaphorique qui s'établit entre mépris et maladie, cette dernière peut être aussi bien comparant implicite d'un comparé explicite mépris (*Lettres de la Duchesse*) que comparé implicite d'un comparant, lui aussi implicite, mépris (histoire d'Amine). L'ambiguïté crébillonienne n'est donc pas limitée aux champs éthique, grammatical et stylistique. Elle étend son emprise aux rapports entre signifiants et signifiés, et ce par un double mode d'action: en exploitant, tout d'abord, toutes les possibilités offertes par diverses homonymies consacrées par l'usage courant (cf. les divers sens du verbe "tomber"), ainsi que par une quasi-homonymie fondée sur la paronomase ("prouver-éprouver"; "tendre-éteindre-attendre"); enfin en utilisant un langage codé où les signifiants particuliers à une isotopie donnée renvoient cette fois à des signifiés relevant d'une isotopie quasiment antithétique à la première. Trois possibilités, donc: un signifiant assorti de signifiés multiples, un signifié global distribué sur des signifiants en relation d'homonymie partielle, enfin un rapport à quatre—car les signifiants du langage codé sont, bien sûr, dotés d'un signifié, de même que les signifiés de ce langage ont eux-mêmes leurs signifiants particuliers. De plus, et dans ce dernier cas, il est clair que la métaphore dont on a dégagé plus haut la discrète présence, repose sur une homologie du type suivant:

maladie : corps physique :: mépris : corps mondain
: (esprit individuel)

Une telle constatation permet de délimiter plus clairement les rapports unissant, dans *Le Hasard*, mépris et maladie. Les maladies physiques (de nature non vénérienne) y concrétisent une possibilité de réintégration de la zone estime pour les tiers au profit desquels elles s'insèrent dans la chaîne causale: telles la maladie de la mère de la Marquise et celle, fatale, de Prévanes. Il apparaît d'autre part que la chaise longue de Célie pointe doublement vers une maladie physique passée et la récurrence prochaine de la maladie morale mépris: elle connote à la fois la convalescence et la galanterie et constitue de ce fait le point crucial où vont converger les deux axes métaphorique et métonymique.

Quant à son occupante, Célie la femme galante et ses incarnations métaphoriques possibles—la courtisane du récit "réaliste," la fée du conte merveilleux parodique[28]—elle révèle encore plus clairement sa participation à la thématique du *gift*, don empoisonné—don-poison—propre au conte merveilleux, mais aussi, dans la perspective libertine-optimiste propre au

Hasard, don-remède: face à la Duchesse des *Lettres* qui, mortellement contaminée par le mépris du monde que son amant a reversé sur elle, choisit l'exil d'un éternel silence—face à la femme empoisonnée, Célie est au contraire, à un degré moindre que la Madame de Li*** des mêmes *Lettres,* femme-poison dont la contagion tue si on tente de la garder (mort de Prévanes), mais aussi femme-potion, femme-vaccin dont l'inoculation permet au corps mondain et à ses mebres d'accroître leur résistance aux atteintes du mal qui les investit.

CONCLUSION

Dans une perspective purement sémiotique, il convient alors de procéder à un réaménagement du carré de sens proposé dans la première partie de cette étude et de transformer ce qui n'était qu'un schéma logique, où s'opposaient les systèmes de valeurs propres à chacun des sexes, en un schéma proprement sémiotique, où chaque déixis et les contenus qu'elle véhicule constituera le lieu où s'investira une isotopie à la fois contraire et complémentaire de celle que propose sa contrepartie. Soit:

1. Carré logique, articulé en fonction des valeurs qui s'incarnent dans les protagonistes de chaque sexe, dans les relations d'attraction et d'antagonisme qui s'établissent entre eux:

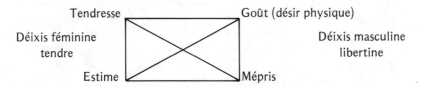

2. Carré sémiotique, résultant de l'analyse du discours proprement dit et obtenu grâce à une rotation partielle des contenus de 1. S'y opposent une déixis où les contenus investis relèvent de la sphère des qualifications éthiques et morales et une déixis dont les contenus s'inscrivent dans le champ des qualifications d'ordre libidinal au sens le plus large:

Ce carré définitif propose les relations suivantes:

(a) Implication mutuelle du désir physique et du mépris: chez Crébillon le mépris n'est pas opérationnel en l'absence de désir physique, et vice-versa.

(b) Implication simple entre le mépris et l'estime, l'estime de soi impliquant—étant achetée, pourrait-on dire, par le mépris de l'autre (cf. le rapport liant l'une à l'autre la Marquise et la Célie du *Hasard*).

(c) Les deux données précédentes confirment à leur tour ce dont on pouvait se douter: la tendresse implique la présence du désir physique; il n'est pas de tendresse véritable sans attraction concomitante des corps, et le platonisme n'est qu'un leurre.

N.B. Les contradictoires estime et désir physique sont liés l'un à l'autre par un rapport secondaire d'identité, quant au bénéficiaire réel de la qualification qu'ils représentent (soi-même), et par un rapport secondaire de contradiction, quant à l'isotopie temporelle dans laquelle ils s'inscrivent en théorie: l'estime est du côté de la durée, le désir du côté de l'instantanéité du moment. Quant aux contradictoires tendresse et mépris, le rapport secondaire d'identité qui les unit est lié au fait que tous deux sont orientés vers un autre, bénéficiaire; le rapport secondaire de contradiction est, lui aussi, inscrit dans l'isotopie temporelle: la tendresse relève de la durée, le mépris de l'instantanéité.

Telle est la complète interdépendance liant les uns aux autres les quatre termes du nouveau carré: on ne peut ici estimer sans aimer, et vice-versa; mais la tendresse impliquant à son tour le désir physique est elle-même indissolublement liée, sur le plan syntagmatique, à son paradigmatique, le mépris de l'autre: ce n'est qu'en passant par le boudoir de Célie que le Duc peut espérer retrouver la Marquise.

NOTES

Introduction

1. Voir en particulier Peter V. Conroy, Jr., *Crébillon fils: Techniques of the Novel*, Studies on Voltaire and the Eighteenth Century, 99 (Banbury, 1972).

2. Voir *Les Paradoxes du romancier: Les "Egarements" de Crébillon*, par un collectif de chercheurs des Universités de Grenoble, Lyon et Saint-Etienne sous la direction de Pierre Rétat (Grenoble: Presses Universitaires de Grenoble, 1975).

3. Bernadette Fort, *Le Langage de l'ambiguïté dans l'œuvre de Crébillon fils* (Paris: Klincksieck, 1978).

4. Ibid., p. 204.

Première Partie

Chapitre I

1. Joseph Courtès, *Introduction à la sémiotique narrative et discursive* (Paris: Hachette, 1976), p. 61.

2. Ibid.

3. Algirdas J. Greimas, *Sémantique structurale* (Paris: Larousse, 1966), pp. 196-97.

4. Ainsi sur un champ de bataille la présence de flocons de fumée est indice d'explosions.

Chapitre II

1. Pour la définition et le fonctionnement du système actantiel, on consultera Courtès, *Introduction*, pp. 60-64.

2. Encore, à défaut de reddition physique actuelle, la Duchesse s'est-elle résolue à voir—et chez Crébillon, voir c'est, d'une certaine façon, succomber—celui qu'elle aime au moment où la conduite de son amant va les séparer à jamais. Quant à l'Hortense des *Egarements*, on peut se demander si l'inachèvement du roman n'a pas contribué à la mettre à l'abri du sort commun.

3. Le mari n'est ici que le représentant de la société, avec qui la femme a en fait passé contrat de mariage.

4. La mère de Meilcour a déjà choisi une épouse à son fils.

5. Si le récit parodique se joue des conventions propres aux genres romanesque et merveilleux, il doit, pour aboutir pleinement, non seulement jouer avec elles, mais encore en renforcer préalablement l'empire.

6. Clifton Cherpack, *An Essay on Crébillon fils* (Durham, N.C.: Duke Univ. Press, 1962), p. 176.

7. Cf. le Nassés et le Mazulhim du *Sopha*, la Madame de Li*** des *Lettres de la Duchesse*. On verra d'autre part que les femmes les plus "estimables" n'en jouent pas moins, chez Crébillon, un jeu parfois fort curieux.

8. C'est peut-être en fonction de cette analyse que s'explique la curieuse attribution d'un prénom traditionnellement féminin au héros de l'épisode.

9. Dans le domaine matériel, l'amour parfait se manifeste également par l'obsession du don ou de la consomption-consumation totale: "que j'étais désespérée qu'il y eût entre nous tant d'égalité, et de trouver si peu à faire en l'épousant. Qu'il eût été doux pour mon amour de le voir en me donnant à lui, me devoir tout, ou de pouvoir lui sacrifier tout ce que je ne pourrais point partager" (*H.O.*, p. 182).

10. Pour la distinction entre jonction, d'une part, disjonction et conjonction, de l'autre, cf. Courtès, *Introduction*, p. 65.

11. La continuation n'est pas plus signifiante que la rupture. Ou plutôt, ces termes n'ont pas cours dans la zone goût: se quitter ne constitue pas plus une rupture que se garder ne correspond à l'exécution fidèle d'un contrat à exécution continue, étalée dans la durée.

12. Cf. les développements consacrés par Bernadette Fort, dans *Le Langage de l'ambiguïté*, à l'énonciation indirecte, et tout particulièrement (pp. 142-53) à la présentation indirecte de la pensée: le recours aux verbes énonciatifs, à la négation, à la litote et à l'hypothétique font de l'énonciateur crébillonien le spectateur des énoncés qu'il émet, et qu'il considère avec autant d'incrédulité que les phénomènes de l'univers sensible qui l'entoure.

13. L'adultère royal était lui-même obligatoirement soumis à publicité: la maîtresse en titre devait être présentée au souverain en présence de la Cour après avoir été dûment mariée (comme la veine "réaliste" de Crébillon, le référentiel exclut le concubinage simple: l'adultère est prescrit).

14. L'Alcibiade des *Lettres athéniennes*, ultime roman de Crébillon, admet cependant l'existence de femmes qui "s'adressent à la tête" et donc à une imagination cette fois masculine.

15. Tout contrat de tendresse rompu s'analysant, rappelons-le, comme relevant *a posteriori* du champ du goût.

16. Le verbe devant être pris au sens juridique strict: conversion d'une valeur mobilière—traditionnellement considérée comme d'un rang inférieur—en bien foncier.

17. Cf., dans le champ politique proprement dit, les *Lettres athéniennes*. La lettre XXIV, de Périclès à Alcibiade, porte essentiellement sur la façon dont le dictateur athénien a littéralement acheté la victoire de sa cité sur les généraux spartiates: "dans cette occasion, ce n'était pas du sang des citoyens, mais de leur or qu'il fallait payer la victoire" (*L.A.*, p. 595).

18. Cf. Kibedi A. Varga, "La Désintégration de l'idéal classique dans le roman français de la première moitié du XVIIIe siècle," *Studies on Voltaire and the Eighteenth Century*, 26 (1963), 965-98. La guerre devenant partie de l'amour, "elle n'est plus véritablement guerre: il n'en reste que la défaite, convenue et sue d'avance. Toute résistance est fonction de la défaite: la guerre devient jeu, on ne résiste que pour succomber" (p. 994). Oui, mais encore faut-il s'entendre sur le jeu auquel on va jouer, ainsi que sur les modalités selon lesquelles s'effectuera la reddition: la lutte subsiste; son objet s'est déplacé.

19. Alibis qui, nous le verrons, passent par la référence à des aventures concernant des tiers, et complaisamment narrées par au moins l'une des parties en présence.

20. Périphérique en ce qu'elle apparaît peu jusqu'aux *Lettres athéniennes*. Elle apparaît toujours cependant en des points stratégiques, et on verra que ces apparitions contribuent en fait à renforcer, en l'explicitant, la logique du système crébillonien dans son ensemble.

21. Parole agressive, persuasive pour l'homme, défensive, argumentative pour la femme qui, comme la Blanchette de Daudet, tente de rester fidèle à un récit-modèle dans lequel, si le loup mange toujours la chèvre, ce n'est pas avant le matin.

22. Insertion qui résulte en fait de leur mise en présence: le "monde" crébillonien doit son existence à l'étincelle produite par le rapprochement des deux systèmes bien plus qu'il ne les contient.

23. Algirdas J. Greimas, *Du sens* (Paris: Seuil, 1970), p. 192; Courtès, *Introduction*, pp. 77-78.

24. Notons dès à présent que la tendre se réjouit de l'impuissance—tout au moins momentanée—de son amant, en ce que celle-ci la rassure sur l'authenticité de la tendresse que celui-ci lui voue (cf., par exemple, *Sopha*, p. 151).

25. Peter Brooks, *The Novel of Worldliness* (Princeton: Princeton Univ. Press, 1969), p. 22. Cf. également l'importance accordée par Brooks à un regard qui fixe l'autre en un véritable *en-soi* sartrien et permet en même temps de se fixer soi-même en un rôle rassurant ou avantageux.

26. L'inachèvement des *Heureux Orphelins* lui ayant interdit de jouer le rôle qui lui revenait de droit et aurait sans doute constitué le point culminant de la triplication narrative selon laquelle se déroulent les exploits amoureux du héros: conquête relativement aisée et rapide de la sage Suffolk; assujettiseement de l'hypocrite Rindsey, d'un prix plus grand, compte tenu des handicaps dont Chester l'assortit lui-même; la lutte contre Pembrook promettait, elle, d'être une lutte à armes égales entre deux champions également maîtres de leur art.

27. Patrick Wald Lasowski, "Le Désir et la civilité dans l'œuvre de Crébillon," *Revue des Sciences Humaines*, 166 (1977), 283.

28. Ibid.

29. Ibid.

30. Philip Stewart, *Le Masque et la parole: Le langage de l'amour au XVIIIe siècle* (Paris: Corti, 1973), p. 176.

Deuxième Partie

Section A

1. Greimas, *Sémantique*, p. 197.

2. Courtès, *Introduction*, p. 75.

3. Ibid., pp. 75 et 79.

4. Greimas, *Sémantique*, pp. 193-94.

5. François, duc de La Rochefoucauld, *La Justification de l'amour*, ed. J.D. Hubert (Paris: Nizet, 1971), p. 64.

6. Cf. *Sopha*, p. 76.

7. Dans une perspective purement ethnologique, elle permettrait sans doute au chercheur d'élargir le débat, en tentant de dégager dans quelle mesure l'amour hors mariage tel qu'il se manifeste dans la littérature du XVIIIe siècle ne constitue pas, en fait, un masque sous lequel se dissimulent des structures fondamentales régissant les fonctions érotiques et sexuelles dans leur généralité la plus vaste. Tel est d'ailleurs l'un des buts que se proposera la dernière partie de cette étude.

8. Henri Lafon, "Les Décors et les choses dans les romans de Crébillon," *Poétique*, 16 (1973), 455-65. Article de premier ordre, dans lequel on consultera avec profit, p. 463, le schéma des commerces possibles, en fonction de leur degré d'intimité, entre les personnages.

9. Roland Barthes, *Fragments d'un discours amoureux* (Paris: Seuil, 1977), p. 228.

10. Le sexe étant pertinent ici.

11. Le verbe "reconnaître" devant être pris au sens de "to perceive" ainsi qu'à celui de "to acknowledge." Reconnaissance impliquant ici le silence de la femme.

12. Cf. la citation de la p. 209 du *Hasard* donnée plus haut.

13. Nous entendons par là le "monde" en tant que lieu de discours, de parole, et la parole en tant que milieu où baigne et au sein duquel évolue l'individu.

Section B

1. Greimas, *Sémantique*, p. 202.

2. Ibid. (c'est nous qui soulignons).

3. Ibid., p. 209.

4. Dans l'économie crébillonienne, les objets-valeurs sont en nombre fini.

5. Greimas, *Sémantique*, p. 209.

6. Barthes, *Fragments*, pp. 183 et 179.

7. "Quoi, vous m'aimerez, vous me le direz!" (*Egarements*, p. 11).

8. Gilles Deleuze, *Proust et les signes* (Paris: P.U.F., 1964), p. 39.

9. On notera que dans certains cas, où tout le plaisir ressenti par la femme l'est dans son imagination—telle l'Araminte de *La Nuite et le moment*—la victoire de l'homme consiste à prendre conscience de la fraude de sa partenaire. Dans les deux cas, la femme est déchiffrée, contrainte qu'elle est de révéler la nature et l'objet de son vouloir au regard de l'autre.

10. On rappellera que la réplique de Célie, p. 166, a valeur d'antiphrase: "la seule félicité qui me reste est le spectacle de la vôtre. Puisse-t-elle être aussi durable que vous le méritez." Les pleurs de la jeune femme ont une signification aussi ambiguë que le comparatif d'égalité qui donne sa structure à la deuxième phrase de sa déclaration, et rappelle immanquablement le "puissiez-vous, s'il se peut, m'aimer autant que vous êtes aimée vous-même," par lequel Clitandre clôt le dialogue de *La Nuit et le moment* (p. 150). Mais ici, l'action subséquente va lever l'ambiguïté initiale.

Section C

1. Greimas, *Sémantique*, p. 198.

2. Ibid., p. 194.

3. Vladimir Propp, *Morphology of the Folktale* (Austin: Univ. of Texas Press, 1973), pp. 39, 50 et 55.

4. Lafon, "Les Décors," p. 463.

5. Comme le Duc accompagnait la Marquise à son carrosse, il donne également la main à Célie pour la conduire au fauteuil. Symétrie qu'on se contente de noter ici, et sur laquelle on reviendra ultérieurement.

Section D

1. Greimas, *Sémantique*, pp. 199-200.
2. Ibid., p. 199.
3. Ibid., p. 201.
4. Ibid., p. 200.
5. Cf., dans les *Lettres athénniennes*, le dénouement de la liaison entre Alcibiade et Aspasie. Si l'homme peut se permettre d'être quitté, c'est ou bien qu'une telle liaison a été tenue secrète vis-à-vis du public, ou encore que la réputation du libertin est telle que ce même public soit à même de comprendre de quoi il retourne.
6. Dans une perspective purement libertine—et l'on retrouve ici l'ambiguïté crébillonienne, on peut dire également que c'est la mort qui sauve Prévanes du ridicule qu'il y a à soigner avec constance une femme qui ne vous aime pas réellement et s'apprête d'ores et déjà à vous donner un successeur: si le ridicule ne tue pas, il vaut mieux, dans un certain sens, être mort que d'y prêter.
7. Voir plus haut, pp. 85-87.
8. Peut-être la révélation, la preuve, relève-t-elle de l'isotopie "message," mais le plaisir éprouvé relève, lui, de l'isotopie "nature héroïque." On notera d'autre part le jeu possible sur les signifiants *éprouver* (au double sens de soumettre à épreuve et ressentir) et *prouver* (au sens particulier de rendre le caché manifeste). Il s'agit bien d'une paire fondamentale, en ce sens que l'essentiel de l'œuvre de Crébillon tourne précisément autour de la dualité fatidique entre être-éprouver et paraître-*ne pas* prouver. Quant à l'épreuve, elle est à la fois scientifique et féerique; *La Nuit et le moment* illustre d'ailleurs à la perfection la première composante du terme, alors que *Le Hasard* en illustre plus précisément la seconde, ainsi qu'on le verra plus loin.
9. Barthes, *Fragments*, pp. 217-19.
10. Cf. *H.O.*, pp. 268-69: "un homme quitté, donne rarement l'envie de le prendre . . . il lui faut encore plus de temps pour leur [aux femmes] faire oublier cette infortune, qu'il n'en a eu besoin lui-même pour s'en consoler, quelque vive qu'ait été la douleur qu'il en a ressentie." Ridicule: allongement de la période au terme de laquelle l'homme peut être repris.
11. Et c'est pour cela que doit être maintenu à tout prix le contrat d'amitié mondaine par lequel la Marquise couvre les activités amoureuses de Célie vis-à-vis de la mère de celle-ci. Célie en exil, Célie recluse dans un couvent, et tout le système s'écroule.
12. Car si D'Alinteuil doit *moins* circuler, il doit cependant *rester* en circulation.
13. Cf. également Fort, précité, dont la brillante analyse du style rocaille en tant qu'évasion du système classique, nous semble par trop laisser dans l'ombre le visage second de ce même style, c'est-à-dire celui d'une exacerbation du système légué au XVIIIe siècle par le siècle précédent.
14. *Encyclopaedia universalis* (Paris: Encyclopaedia Universalis, S.A., 1968), article "Aristote," I, 398.

Section E

1. Platon, *Oeuvres*, éd. et trad. E. Chambry (Paris: Garnier, 1922), p. 221.
2. Ibid., p. 219.

3. "Puissiez-vous, s'il se peut, m'aimer autant que vous êtes aimée vous-même."

4. Il serait intéressant de procéder à une comparaison, tant sur le plan de la grammaire narrative que dans un contexte économique, entre récit libertin et récit-histoire de vampires.

5. Rutherford, M.R. de Labriolle, "L'Evolution de la notion de luxe depuis Mandeville jusqu'à la Révolution," *Studies on Voltaire and the Eighteenth Century*, 26 (1963), 1028-36.

6. "Ce sont les passions qui sont à l'origine de l'activité humaine qui facilite le fonctionnement de l'état" (ibid., p. 1032).

7. Louise K. Horowitz, *Love and Language: A Study of the Classical French Moralists* (Columbus: Ohio State Univ. Press, 1977), p. 7; nous traduisons.

8. Jacques Rochette, chevalier de la Morlière, *Angola* (Paris: Flammarion, 1895), p. 111. *Angola* date de 1749. Dès 1741, le jeune héros de Duclos rendait l'une de ses conquêtes à la société, à la demande de l'un des soupirants de la dame, réduit à l'inaction par la ténacité du goût de celle-ci: "je sentis tous mes torts, je songeai à les réparer, et je rendis dans le jour même à la société comme un effet qui devait être dans le commerce" (Duclos, *Confessions du Comte de . . .*, dans *Romanciers du XVIIIe siècle* [Paris: Pléiade, 1965], II, 267-68).

9. En ce sens que l'apparence de lutte au terme de laquelle l'hypocrite se "donne" à son séducteur recouvre une lutte réelle, dont l'objet est le prix que chacun attache à l'acquisition de ce qu'il désire.

10. Il existe un point, non déterminé, où l'excès de circulation de la femme menace ses partenaires éventuels d'une dévaluation quasi-irrécupérable: tel D'Alinteuil, définitivement condamné aux Célie et aux Valsy, aux ruptures quasi-instantanées et aux longues périodes de mise en disponibilité forcée.

11. Tel le Clitandre de *La Nuit et le moment*.

12. Célie en tant qu'acteur dans lequel s'investissent les objets-valeurs "homologues" dans des isotopies différentes, "mépris" et "circulation."

13. Parler à Célie (interlocution), parler de Célie (délocution). Parole qui s'incarne dans les acteurs que sont le Duc et la Marquise. La délocution joue un rôle essentiel dans l'articulation du dialogue: c'est au cours de la conversation qu'ils tiennent sur Célie que se complète le portrait de celle-ci et qu'apparaissent des possibilités de développements ultérieurs. Là encore, "le 'sujet' vient au monde par le potin" (Barthes, *Fragments*, p. 218).

14. Dans le monde selon Crébillon, on devient, en somme, ce que l'on est. Ce monde, où le regard des autres exerce sa tyrannie, c'est sans aucun doute l'empire de l'*en-soi* sartrien, où le public, à la satisfaction de tous (sauf de celles qui s'investissent tout entières et aveuglément dans la tendresse), a pour responsabilité de faire passer au plan de la performance ce qui reste improductivement bloqué et thésaurisé à celui de la compétence.

15. Une fois de plus, précise mystérieusement le texte par la bouche de Célie: "Ce n'est pas là le premier tour que Madame sa mère me joue" (*Has.*, p. 189).

Troisième Partie

Introduction

1. Lafon, "Les Décors," pp. 455-68.
2. Ibid., p. 457.

3. *La Nuit et le moment* exploite également le motif de l'influence des "climats": l'un des récits enchâssés, la double aventure de Clitandre et de Julie, tourne autour du dissentiment initial des deux acteurs: dans quelle mesure la chaleur extérieure affecte-t-elle les capacités amoureuses de l'homme? Dans le récit enchâssant lui-même, c'est en prétextant du froid que Clitandre s'introduit dans le lit de Cidalise.

Chapitre I

1. Lafon, "Les Décors," p. 460.

2. Cf., par exemple, Rosalie de Watteville dans l'*Albert Savarus* de Balzac.

3. On peut d'ailleurs ajouter à la connotation "non-productivité spectaculaire," la connotation "gâchage": l'étoffe ainsi gaspillée est généralement précieuse.

4. *Egar.*, p. 106.

5. Lequel englobe Versailles, dont l'un des sèmes fondamentaux est bien évidemment antithétique à "intimité." Quant au froid, au stade actuel de cette lecture, il peut correspondre au froid physique d'un palais dont on ne peut chauffer convenablement les pièces d'*apparat* (froid figuré de l'étiquette).

6. Célie s'étonne de ce que Norsan ait pu courir après des *espèces* "qui n'auraient pas seulement mérité l'attention du moins délicat de ses valets de chambre" (*Has.*, p. 210). A quoi le Duc répond: "On est souvent étonné, à la guerre, de voir un grand général s'amuser à prendre des bicoques, parce qu'on ignore ses projets, et par conséquent, le prix qu'il attache à des conquêtes qui paraissent si peu faites pour le tenter. Il en est de même de M. de Norsan: on voit ce qu'il fait; mais on n'en pénètre pas le motif" (pp. 210-11). Soit l'homologie général:bicoques::Norsan:espèces.

7. "... il semble que Prométhée m'ait livré son secret" (p. 262).

8. *La Nuit et le moment* contient, dans l'épisode de Julie, une esquisse du système rhétorique et logique dont nous nous proposons de faire ici l'étude. On se référera à la déclaration de Clitandre, p. 164: "Elle [Julie] en vint enfin jusqu'à me soutenir que ce jour-là notamment [jour de chaleur excessive], il n'y avait point d'homme . . . qui ne se trouvât absolument *éteint*" (c'est nous qui soulignons).

9. Il nous appartiendra, dans des développements ultérieurs, de vérifier l'hypothèse déjà formulée, selon laquelle chez Crébillon il se peut qu'on ne désire sexuellement que ce que l'on méprise.

10. Ce jeu vient s'ajouter à celui, dégagé dans la première partie de cette étude, entre "prouver" et les deux significations d' "éprouver," jeu dont on a vu l'importance au niveau d'une dénomination des diverses épreuves.

11. Il serait tentant d'adjoindre à cette triade fondamentale un quatrième signifiant, attesté à la p. 242: le Duc, tentant de se mettre à l'abri des tentatives de séduction dont l'accable Célie, "prend un air et un ton *attendris*" pour parler de l'amant défunt de la jeune femme.

12. Lequel est à la fois techniquement "froid" et officiellement "feu". . . .

13. Ironie qui ne sera pas perdue pour Laclos. Ironie qui d'autre part revêt une ambiguïté aux multipes facettes: de quel(s) temps s'agit-il? Et qui parle? Meilcour, "l'auteur fictif" des *Egarements*, ou Crébillon lui-même?

14. Non sans une perte symbolique de sa lucidité: cf. le "mes flambeaux s'éteignirent" de la p. 204.

15. Et d'autant plus incisive que Célie admet elle-même qu'elle en a été exemptée lors de sa première rencontre avec Norsan.

16. On notera la possibilité d'une chaîne logique qui s'établirait entre feu, suisse

et grison, ce dernier étant soit un domestique vêtu de gris, soit un citoyen du canton suisse du même nom; quant aux ramoneurs, rappelons qu'ils venaient traditionnellement de Savoie.

17. Cf. p. 227: "Ici la conversation tombe, une minute à peu près: et Célie paraît rêver assez profondément." Cf. également p. 240: "le Duc paraît tomber dans une rêverie assez profonde."

18. Cf. p. 160: "Tout ce qui nous [les femmes] heurte ne nous fait pas tomber."

19. Cité par Joseph Courtès, dans *Lévi-Strauss et les contraintes de la pensée mythique* (Paris: Mame, 1973), p. 95.

20. Mais dont il n'a peut-être pas encore pleinement pris conscience en ce qui le concerne.

21. Célie était également responsable du "il doit être gelé" de la p. 169, par lequel elle suscitait, dans le discours, la présence d'un corps masculin—celui du Duc.

22. Les lois thermiques et celles de la vraisemblance sont donc invoquées par deux fois, et en deux points cruciaux du dialogue: dans l'adresse du narrateur au lecteur, avant que ne s'ouvre la scène 5 et, avant que n'explose le moment, dans ce court débat opposant le Duc à Célie.

23. Sans doute le discours séducteur est-il discours d'action, donc procès, mais il participe aussi d'un état de conversation, dont les italiques symbolisent l'acte-saut qui rend possible de s'en évader. Le récit libertin semble d'ailleurs fournir un curieux équivalent narratif de l'hypothèse émise par Zénon d'Elée, selon laquelle Achille serait impuissant à rattraper la tortue qui le précède: il découpe le temps-durée en fragments de plus en plus ténus, constitutifs du rituel de séduction, jusqu'au point où seul un saut qualitatif est susceptible d'assurer la conjonction sexuelle désirée ou redoutée: saut que symbolise le recours aux italiques.

24. Les passages entre guillemets figurant dans cette énumération sont des citations tirées des pp. 247-49 du dialogue.

25. Des trois protagonistes, le discours de Célie est d'ailleurs celui qui recourt le plus, même dans les premières scènes, aux modes interrogatif et interjectif. Le désordre parataxique qui l'imprègne toujours plus ou moins, s'oppose de façon frappante à la *dispositio* impeccable du texte affecté au Duc et à la Marquise.

26. Immobilité anormale en tant que l'homme dans la force de l'âge est normalement non fixé, tant dans la sphère d'activité monaine et/ou libertine que dans l'espace mondain d'un salon ou d'un boudoir. Seul le petit-maître se vautre dans des fauteuils normalement réservés aux femmes et aux hommes âgés, une telle conduite connotant jusqu'à un certain point la "non-virilité" du sujet. Quant à la mobilité outrée de Célie, elle est à la fois anormale sur le plan de la conduite mondaine (elle relève en fait de la gestuelle de la tragédie, d'où son effet comique), mais parfaitement révélatrice dans le cadre de la théorie du mouvement élaborée plus haut. Il ne reste plus au Duc qu'à greffer la circularité d'un tel déplacement sur celle du circuit de l'échange libertin-mondain.

27. Zone du froid-mépris à laquelle on a vu qu'appartient également Versailles: par son slimat, par ses mœurs.

28. Le dialogue pourrait avoir pour sous-titre, au choix: "Comment Célie, ayant dîné avec la Marquise, soupa avec le Duc," ou encore "Comment le Duc, n'ayant pas dîné avec la Marquise, soupa avec Célie." Pour les allusions aux repas pris ou sautés, voir *Has.*, pp. 169, 180 et 286. Pour la place accordée à la nourriture chez Crébillon, voir également l'excellent article de Philippe Berthier, "Le Souper impossible," dans *Les Paradoxes du romancier: Les "Egarements,"* éd. Pierre Rétat (Grenoble: Presses Universitaires de Grenoble, 1975), pp. 75-88.

Chapitre II

1. Et à la rédaction de celui-ci, comme en témoigne la présence du terme "persiflage" dans la réplique: "Ah! Vous voulez ressusciter le persiflage, c'est un projet!" (*Has.*, p. 215). Or, ce n'est que dans les années cinquante que ce mot fait son apparition, avec le verbe "persifler." Célie parle d'ailleurs de "ressusciter" le persiflage, indiquant ainsi que la rédaction du dialogue date du début des années soixante, période où "la gravité aura succédé au badinage et une ostentation d'honnêteté à l'humeur maligne, dans le ton général de la société." (Jean Fabre, *Idées sur le roman, de Madame de Lafayette au Marquis de Sade* [Paris: Klincksieck, 1979], p. 147). *Le Hasard* est donc postérieur de 26 ans à *La Nuit et le moment*, publiée en 1755, mais dont la rédaction remonte à 1737.

2. Cf. la Table des éditions citées, en tête de volume.

3. Madame d'Auneuil, *La Tyrannie des fées détruite*, dans *Cabinet des fées* (Paris: Club du Meilleur Livre, 1955), II, 317. Voir aussi, dans le même volume, le *Tourbillon* de Mademoiselle de la Force, où le jeune génie du même nom préfigure le héros-sylphe libertin de Crébillon, ainsi que le conte allégorique *Sans parangon* de Preschac, où la bonne et la mauvaise fée se révèlent être la même personne.

4. Cf. *Egar.*, pp. 259, 271. Les porte-parole en question peuvent d'ailleurs être aussi bien l'homme (libertin: le Versac des *Egarements* dans l'ordre mondain) que la femme (sage et lucide: la Sultane du *Sopha* dans l'ordre littéraire).

5. On doit considérer que le procès constitue l'équivalent "réaliste" de l'épreuve propre au genre féerique. On peut d'ailleurs y voir un indice textuel de la dégradation du statut des membres masculins de la classe noble dans la sphère référentielle: là où le héros de roman ou de féerie, image idéalisée de la fonction guerrière traditionnellement réservée à la noblesse d'épée, livre lui-même ses combats armés sous la protection de pouvoirs surnaturels, le "héros" mondain en est réduit à subir les aléas d'un procès, et à dépendre du bon vouloir des membres de la classe parlementaire et des entremises de sa maîtresse. On se reportera, pour confirmation, aux *Lettres de la Marquise*, p. 438, où le Comte est lui-même partie à un procès qui le retient éloigné de l'héroïne: "tous les procès du monde valent-ils celui que je pourrais vous faire perdre?" Dans un autre lettre (48, p. 518), la Marquise apprend à son amant qu'elle a "fait l'emplette d'un petit magistrat" digne "d'effacer Céladon," et conclut, en taquinant le Comte: "que les armes cèdent à la magistrature."

6. Tout comme le système éthique cornélien dont il dérive partiellement, le système crébillonien tend à se durcir au cours de la seconde moitié de l'œuvre, en même temps qu'il élargit son champ d'action, jusqu'à s'appliquer, dans les *Lettres athéniennes*, à la sphère politique.

7. C'est le problème posé par la "sensibilité" de la femme et sa possible antinomie par rapport à la "décence," dont il est débattu à loisir dans *La Nuit et le moment* (pp. 92-95).

8. La Duchesse est plus stricte que la Marquise du *Hasard*: il est inélégant de repasser à un ami une femme dont on ne sait plus que faire (*Duch.*, p. 30). Mais il faut tenir compte de ce que ses *Lettres* occupent le versant "moral" de l'œuvre de Crébillon, où les distinctions entre tendresse et caprice sont moins fermes. Ainsi de M. de Cercey, "bénéficiaire" théorique de l'abandonnée: "Il ne serait pas le premier à qui le caprice et l'occasion aient tenu lieu de goût." On notera le glissement sémantique du dernier terme, ici l'équivalent probable de "penchant sérieux."

9. L'aventure de Chester et de Madame Rindsey dans *Les Heureux Orphelins*

témoigne assez que l'entreprise de séduction libertine n'est ici, compte tenu de l'objet choisi et des péripéties dont le séducteur l'assortit, qu'une vengeance à retardement: Rindsey paie pour toutes les autres.

10. Non seulement le mépris est indissociable du désir sexuel, mais il s'accroît en proportion inverse de la distance séparant ceux qui en sont le sujet et l'objet: les outrages que le Duc fait subir à la Duchesse s'aggravent au fur et à mesure que celle-ci est plus près de s'abandonner à son amour pour lui, comme en témoignent à la fois ses goûts successifs ainsi que le scandale croissant qui les accompagne.

11. A l'inverse, quel était le motif réel de sa reddition partielle? La force invisible de l'amour, ou l'irrésistible fascination qu'exerce progressivement sur l'héroïne le mépris dont est imprégnée toute la conduite du Duc?

12. On notera que dans les deux œuvres, la protagoniste se dispose à livrer une jeune fille innocente à un libertin. Il est vrai que la Duchesse se propose ce beau résultat par l'intermédiaire d'un mariage en due forme . . . .

13. *Tyrannie*, p. 363.

14. Madame d'Auneuil épargne une seule fée, Serpente, dont la personnalité et les fonctions qui lui seront dévolues auprès de la jeune libératrice sentent fort, elles aussi, l'allégorisation de la figure historique de Madame de Maintenon, survivante de l'ère du libertinage royal et des "enchantements" versaillais, mais devenue le support actif du catholicisme en même temps qu'ennemie jurée des fées.

15. En liaison avec le procès perdu par la Marquise, qui désigne l'ordre nouveau comme essentiellement bourgeois.

16. Du moins dans l'univers du référent; dans l'univers littéraire, la fée, discrètement réintroduite et soigneusement masquée, exercera de nouveau son pouvoir ainsi qu'en témoigne la Sanseverina dans le roman à plus d'un titre crébillonien de Stendhal.

17. On retrouve l'alliance indissoluble, fondée sur une double implication, du "méprisable" et du "mépris." Les choix et actions du Duc constituent autant de preuves de mépris à l'égard de la Duchesse, mais aussi autant de raisons pour celle-ci de le mépriser. Les *Lettres athéniennes* développeront d'ailleurs plus à loisir le thème du mépris de la femme pour l'homme, tout particulièrement dans le cadre de la liaison Alcibiade-Aspasie.

18. Dans *Le Hasard*, c'est au contraire l'estime qui fait retour, avec le Duc lui-même.

19. Claude-Michel Cluny, *"La Nuit et le moment,"* *Les Lettres Françaises*, No. 1139 (1966), 13. Jugement auquel il est permis de ne pas souscrire.

20. Le terme anglais parle davantage dans ce contexte particulier que son équivalent français.

21. Dans la perspective générative, il est évident qu'au sein de cet univers libertin le récit constitue l'équivalent de l'enfant absent. Ce que l'on conçoit au cours d'une aventure érotique, c'est essentiellement à la fois une situation de narration ainsi que le narré qui en résultera par la suite: on se raconte des histoires érotiques, puis (et à cause de cette narration) on fait l'amour, et cette aventure se métamorphosera elle-même en un récit qu'on fera circuler. Il est d'ailleurs à noter que lorsque Diderot passe du libertinage des *Bijoux* à l'utopie du *Supplément au Voyage de Bougainville*, il reprend le principe double de génération-circulation pour l'appliquer aux enfants eux-mêmes.

22. *Sopha*, p. 70. On notera le jeu sur les sèmes humain et non humain du terme, ainsi que sur les sèmes totalité et partie. Le "témoin," c'est ici non pas l'être humain chargé d'une déposition quelconque, mais l'organe physique révélateur de symptômes. (Cf. latin: *testis*.)

23. "Commerce" est en quelque sorte l'équivalent (l'homologue) classique du terme "communication" en usage aujourd'hui dans les sciences humaines.

24. Tendresse qui, précise le narrateur, "était à l'épreuve de tout . . ." (*Sopha*, p. 74).

25. Telle est donc, en filigrane, la dégradation qu'inflige cet épisode aux deux divinités tutélaires sous l'égide desquelles nous avions placé la conclusion du précédent chapitre. *Cupidon*, dieu du commerce amoureux dans ce qu'il a de plus gratuit, s'y fait à présent la divinité éponyme de la cupidité la plus matérielle qui soit: le désir érotique a fait place à l'avarice pure et simple. Quant à Hermes-*Mercure*, dieu de la circulation marchande et des médecins, il prête ici son nom au seul élément chimique susceptible de venir à bout d'une maladie vénérienne (et ici vénale). Et Crébillon ouvre la voie à Schnitzler.

26. Amine n'est pas "méprisable" en tant que courtisane—il est, les *Lettres athéniennes* nous l'apprendront, des courtisanes estimables—mais parce qu'elle est incapable d'exécuter fidèlement les contrats auxquels elle est partie. Comme pour la Célie du *Hasard*, il semble que cette incapacité soit fondée sur un manque de logique, consistant à mélanger les catégories: faire payer (sphère de l'économique) en fonction des religions ou des races (sphère physique ou morale).

27. Tout comme le corps peut dissimuler les organes porteurs de symptômes, le texte peut soumettre au même traitement les mots-symptômes eux-mêmes, tel "guérie," cité et analysé plus haut. On notera d'autre part que c'est ce dernier signifiant qui révèle la présence, dans et sous le texte, du signifié maladie, lequel n'apparaîtra donc jamais qu'en creux, par le manque que constitue son antonyme.

28. Il s'agit ici de la fée—personnage explicité par le discours narratif lui-même. On rappellera que dans les *Lettres de la Duchesse*, la "féerie" est présente, mais sousjacente: la "fée" y a emprunté l'enveloppe humaine de la femme.

BIBLIOGRAPHIE

I. Sources principales

Crébillon, Claude Prosper Jolyot de. *Collection complette des œuvres de m. de Crébillon le fils.* Londres: s.l., 1772. Vols. II, IV-VII.
———. *L'Ecumoire, ou Tanzaï et Néadarné, histoire japonaise.* Ed. Ernest Sturm. Paris: Nizet, 1976.
———. *Les Egarements du cœur et de l'esprit, ou les Mémoires de M. de Meilcour.* Ed. Pierre Lièvre. Paris: Le Divan, 1929.
———. *La Nuit et le moment. Le Hasard du coin du feu.* Ed. Pierre Lièvre. Paris: Le Divan, 1929.
———. *Le Sopha, conte moral.* Ed. Pierre Lièvre. Paris: Le Divan, 1930.

II. Sources secondaires

A. Etudes consacrées à Crébillon et au XVIIIe siècle

Baril, Germaine, et Lloyd R. Free. "Antithesis and Synthesis in Crébillon's *Les Egarements du cœur et de l'esprit.*" *South Atlantic Bulletin*, 45, No. 4 (1980), 23-32.
Bennington, Geoff. "From Narrative to Text: Love and Writing in Crébillon fils, Duclos, Barthes." *The Oxford Literary Review*, 4 (1979), 62-81.
Boyer, Henri. "Structuration d'un roman épistolaire: Enonciation et fiction." *Revue des Sciences Humaines*, 80 (1972), 297-327..
Brooks, Peter. *The Melodramatic Imagination.* New Haven et Londres: Yale Univ. Press, 1976.
———. *The Novel of Worldliness.* Princeton: Princeton Univ. Press, 1969.
Cherpack, Clifton. *An Essay on Crébillon fils.* Durham, N.C.: Duke Univ. Press, 1962.
Cluny, Claude-Michel. "*La Nuit et le moment.*" *Les Lettres Françaises*, No. 1139 (1966), 13.

Conroy, Peter V., Jr. *Crébillon fils: Techniques of the Novel.* Banbury, Oxon: Voltaire Foundation, 1972.

Ebel, Miriam. "New Light on the Novelist Crébillon fils." *French Review,* 47, No. 6 (Special Issue) (1974), 38-46.

Fabre, Jean. *Idées sur le roman de Madame de Lafayette au Marquis de Sade.* Paris: Klincksieck, 1979.

Fort, Bernadette. *Le Langage de l'ambiguïté dans l'œuvre de Crébillon fils.* Paris: Klincksieck, 1978.

Girard, Anne. "La Parole soufflée." *Littérature,* 31 (1978), 64-76.

Labrosse, Claude. "Récit romanesque et enquête anthropologique à propos des *Egarements du cœur et de l'esprit.*" Dans *Roman et lumières au XVIIIᵉ siècle: Colloque sous la présidence de MM. Werner Krauss, et al.* Paris: Editions Sociales, 1970, pp. 73-88 et 108-12 (discussion).

Lafon, Henri. "Les Décors et les choses dans les romans de Crébillon." *Poétique,* 16 (1973), 455-65.

Lasowski, Patrick Wald. "Le Désir et la civilité dans l'œuvre de Crébillon." *Revue des Sciences Humaines,* 166 (1977), 281-94.

Mauzi, Robert. *L'Idée du bonheur dans la littérature et la pensée françaises au XVIIIᵉ siècle.* Paris: Armand Colin, 1965.

Nagy, Péter. *Libertinage et révolution.* Paris: Gallimard, 1965.

Palmer, Benjamin W. "Crébillon fils and His Reader." *Studies on Voltaire and the Eighteenth Century,* 132 (1972), 183-97.

Rétat, Pierre, éd. *Les Paradoxes du romancier: Les "Egarements" de Crébillon.* Grenoble: Presses Universitaires de Grenoble, 1975.

Rutherford, M.R. de Labriolle. "L'Evolution de la notion de luxe depuis Mandeville jusqu'à la Révolution." *Studies on Voltaire and the Eighteenth Century,* 26 (1963), 1025-36.

Sarr-Echevin, Thérèse. "L'Esprit de jeu dans l'œuvre de Crébillon fils." *Revue des Sciences Humaines,* 124 (1966), 361-80.

Stewart, Philip. *Le Masque et la parole: Le langage de l'amour au XVIIIᵉ siècle.* Paris: Corti, 1973.

Varga, A. Kibedi. "La Désintégration de l'idéal classique dans le roman français de la première moitié du XVIIIᵉ siècle." *Studies on Voltaire and the Eighteenth Century,* 26 (1963), 965-98.

Versini, Laurent. *Laclos et la tradition: Essai sur les sources et la technique dans les "Liaisons dangereuses."* Paris: Klincksieck, 1968.

B. Autres Ouvrages

Barthes, Roland. *Fragments d'un discours amoureux.* Paris: Seuil, 1977.

———. *S/Z.* Paris: Seuil, 1970.

Bataille, Georges. *L'Erotisme*. Paris: Union Générale d'Editions, 1957.

———. *Histoire de l'érotisme*. Vol. VIII des *Oeuvres complètes*. Paris: Gallimard, 1976.

Bataille: Colloque de Cerisy, 1972. Directeur, Philippe Sollers. Paris: Union Générale d'Editions, 1973.

Brès, Yvon. *La Psychologie de Platon*. Paris: P.U.F., 1968.

Le Cabinet des fées. Ed. André Bay. Paris: Club du Meilleur Livre, 1955.

Courtès, Joseph. *Introduction à la sémiotique narrative et discursive*. Paris: Hachette, 1976.

———. *Lévi-Strauss et les contraintes de la pensée mythique*. Paris: Hachette, 1976.

Deleuze, Gilles. *Proust et les signes*. Paris: P.U.F., 1964.

Dictionnaire des œuvres érotiques, domaine français. Paris: Mercure de France, 1971.

Encyclopaedia universalis. Articles "Aristote," "Crébillon" et "Libertins." Paris: Encyclopaedia Universalis, S.A., 1968.

Flahault, François. *La Parole intermédiaire*. Paris: Seuil, 1978.

Girard, René. *Des Choses cachées depuis la fondation du monde*. Paris: Grasset, 1978.

———. *Critique dans un souterrain*. Lausanne: Editions de l'Age d'Homme, 1976.

———. *Mensonge romantique et vérité romanesque*. Paris: Grasset, 1961.

———. *La Violence et le sacré*. Paris: Grasset, 1972.

Gould, Thomas. *Platonic Love*. New York: The Free Press of Glencoe, 1963.

Greimas, Algirdas J. *Sémantique structurale*. Paris: Larousse, 1966.

———, et Joseph Courtès. *Sémiotique: Dictionnaire raisonné de la théorie du langage*. Paris: Hachette, 1979.

Horowitz, Louise K. *Love and Language: A Study of the Classical French Moralists*. Columbus: Ohio State Univ. Press, 1977.

Koyré, Alexandre. *Introduction à la lecture de Platon*. Paris: Gallimard, 1962.

La Morlière, Jacques Rochette, chevalier de. *Angola*. Paris: Flammarion, 1895.

La Rochefoucauld, François, duc de. *La Justification de l'amour*. Ed. J.D. Hubert. Paris: Nizet, 1971.

Lessing, Gotthold E. *Laocoon*. Trad. Edward Allen McCormick. Indianapolis: Bobbs-Merrill, 1962.

Marignac, Aloys de. *Imagination et dialectique: Essai sur l'expression du spirituel par l'image dans les dialogues de Platon*. Paris: Les Belles Lettres, 1951.

Metz, Christian. *Essais sur la signification au cinéma*. Vol. I. Paris: Klincksieck, 1971.

Niderst, Alain. *Fontenelle à la recherche de lui-même (1657-1702)*. Paris: Nizet, 1972.

Platon. *Oeuvres: Ion, Lisias, Protagoras, Phèdre, Le Banquet*. Trad. E. Chambry. Paris: Garnier, 1922.

Propp, Vladimir. *Morphology of the Folktale*. Austin: Univ. of Texas Press, 1973.

Proust, Marcel. *A la recherche du temps perdu*. Paris: Gallimard, 1954.

Ricardou, Jean. *Nouveaux Problèmes du roman*. Paris: Seuil, 1978.

Romanciers du XVIIIᵉ siècle. Ed. Etiemble. Vol. II. Paris: Corti, 1973.

Rousset, Jean. *Narcisse romancier*. Paris: Corti, 1973.

Starobinski, Jean. "La Rochefoucauld et les morales substitutives." *N.R.F.*, 28 (1966), 16-34, 211-20.

Todorov, Tzvetan. *Poétique de la prose*. Paris: Seuil, 1971.

FRENCH FORUM MONOGRAPHS

1. Karolyn Waterson. *Molière et l'autorité: Structures sociales, structures comiques.* 1976.
2. Donna Kuizenga. *Narrative Strategies in* La Princesse de Clèves. 1976.
3. Ian J. Winter. *Montaigne's Self-Portrait and Its Influence in France, 1580-1630.* 1976.
4. Judith G. Miller. *Theater and Revolution in France since 1968.* 1977.
5. Raymond C. La Charité, ed. *O un amy! Essays on Montaigne in Honor of Donald M. Frame.* 1977.
6. Rupert T. Pickens. *The Welsh Knight: Paradoxicality in Chrétien's* Conte del Graal. 1977.
7. Carol Clark. *The Web of Metaphor: Studies in the Imagery of Montaigne's* Essais. 1978.
8. Donald Maddox. *Structure and Sacring: The Systematic Kingdom in Chrétien's* Erec et Enide. 1978.
9. Betty J. Davis. *The Storytellers in Marguerite de Navarre's* Heptaméron. 1978.
10. Laurence M. Porter. *The Renaissance of the Lyric in French Romanticism: Elegy, "Poëme" and Ode.* 1978.
11. Bruce R. Leslie. *Ronsard's Successful Epic Venture: The Epyllion.* 1979.
12. Michelle A. Freeman. *The Poetics of* Translatio Studii *and* Conjointure: Chrétien de Troyes's Cligés. 1979.
13. Robert T. Corum, Jr. *Other Worlds and Other Seas: Art and Vision in Saint-Amant's Nature Poetry.* 1979.
14. Marcel Muller. *Préfiguration et structure romanesque dans* A la recherche du temps perdu *(avec un inédit de Marcel Proust).* 1979.
15. Ross Chambers. *Meaning and Meaningfulness: Studies in the Analysis and Interpretation of Texts.* 1979.
16. Lois Oppenheim. *Intentionality and Intersubjectivity: A Phenomenological Study of Butor's* La Modification. 1980.
17. Matilda T. Bruckner. *Narrative Invention in Twelfth-Century French Romance: The Convention of Hospitality (1160-1200).* 1980.
18. Gérard Defaux. *Molière, ou les métamorphoses du comique: De la comédie morale au triomphe de la folie.* 1980.
19. Raymond C. La Charité. *Recreation, Reflection and Re-Creation: Perspectives on Rabelais's* Pantagruel. 1980.
20. Jules Brody. *Du style à la pensée: Trois études sur les* Caractères de La Bruyère. 1980.
21. Lawrence D. Kritzman. *Destruction/Découverte: Le Fonctionnement de la rhétorique dans les* Essais de Montaigne. 1980.
22. Minnette Grunmann-Gaudet and Robin F. Jones, eds. *The Nature of Medieval Narrative.* 1980.
23. J.A. Hiddleston. *Essai sur Laforgue et les* Derniers Vers *suivi de Laforgue et Baudelaire.* 1980.
24. Michael S. Koppisch. *The Dissolution of Character: Changing Perspectives in La Bruyère's* Caractères. 1981.
25. Hope H. Glidden. *The Storyteller as Humanist: The* Serées *of Guillaume Bouchet.* 1981.
26. Mary B. McKinley. *Words in a Corner: Studies in Montaigne's Latin Quotations.* 1981.

27. Donald M. Frame and Mary B. McKinley, eds. *Columbia Montaigne Conference Papers.* 1981.
28. Jean-Pierre Dens. *L'Honnête Homme et la critique du goût: Esthétique et société au XVIIe siècle.* 1981.
29. Vivian Kogan. *The Flowers of Fiction: Time and Space in Raymond Queneau's Les Fleurs bleues.* 1982.
30. Michael Issacharoff et Jean-Claude Vilquin, éds. *Sartre et la mise en signe.* 1982.
31. James W. Mileham. *The Conspiracy Novel: Structure and Metaphor in Balzac's Comédie humaine.* 1982.
32. Andrew G. Suozzo, Jr. *The Comic Novels of Charles Sorel: A Study of Structure, Characterization and Disguise.* 1982.
33. Margaret Whitford. *Merleau-Ponty's Critique of Sartre's Philosophy.* 1982.
34. Gérard Defaux. *Le Curieux, le glorieux et la sagesse du monde dans la première moitié du XVIe siècle: L'exemple de Panurge (Ulysse, Démosthène, Empédocle).* 1982.
35. Doranne Fenoaltea. *"Si haulte Architecture." The Design of Scève's* Délie. 1982.
36. Peter Bayley and Dorothy Gabe Coleman, eds. *The Equilibrium of Wit: Essays for Odette de Mourgues.* 1982.
37. Carol J. Murphy. *Alienation and Absence in the Novels of Marguerite Duras.* 1982.
38. Mary Ellen Birkett. *Lamartine and the Poetics of Landscape.* 1982.
39. Jules Brody. *Lectures de Montaigne.* 1982.
40. John D. Lyons. *The Listening Voice: An Essay on the Rhetoric of Saint-Amant.* 1982.
41. Edward C. Knox. *Patterns of Person: Studies in Style and Form from Corneille to Laclos.* 1983.
42. Marshall C. Olds. *Desire Seeking Expression: Mallarmé's "Prose pour des Esseintes."* 1983.
43. Ceri Crossley. *Edgar Quinet (1803-1875): A Study in Romantic Thought.* 1983.
44. Rupert T. Pickens, ed. *The Sower and His Seed: Essays on Chrétien de Troyes.* 1983.
45. Barbara C. Bowen. *Words and the Man in French Renaissance Literature.* 1983.
46. Clifton Cherpack. *Logos in Mythos. Ideas and Early French Narrative.* 1983.
47. Donald Stone, Jr. *Mellin de Saint-Gelais and Literary History.* 1983.
48. Louisa E. Jones. *Sad Clowns and Pale Pierrots: Literature and the Popular Comic Arts in 19th-Century France.* 1984.
49. JoAnn DellaNeva. *Song and Counter-Song: Scève's* Délie *and Petrarch's* Rime. 1983.
50. John D. Lyons and Nancy J. Vickers, eds. *The Dialectic of Discovery: Essays on the Teaching and Interpretation of Literature Presented to Lawrence E. Harvey.* 1984.
51. Warren F. Motte, Jr. *The Poetics of Experiment: A Study of the Work of Georges Perec.* 1984.
52. Jean R. Joseph. *Crébillon fils. Economie érotique et narrative.* 1984.

French Forum, Publishers, Inc.
P.O. Box 5108, Lexington, Kentucky 40505

Publishers of *French Forum*, a journal of literary criticism

2860